Voices from the Kingdom

All God's Children Have Keys

Beverly Cole

Kimimi Publications
PO Box 358
Salina, KS 67402-0358
www.kimimipub.com

Cover Design by Pamela Harris

Cover Photo by Dale K. Cole

Published 2007

Printed by Josten's Printing and Publishing

Printed in the United States

ISBN 0-9788522-0-6
ISBN 978-0-9788522-0-7

Library of Congress Control Number: 2001012345

Also by Beverly Cole from Kimimi Publications:
Cleaning Closets: A Mother's Story – revised edition 2007

Voices from the Kingdom

All God's Children Have Keys

Beverly Cole

Kimimi PUBLICATIONS
Salina, Kansas
www.kimimipub.com

Advance Acclaim for Voices from the Kingdom.

In one of this book's interviews, Jerry says, "I think it's valuable to put a face on the issue." He is exactly right, and Beverly Cole's collection of interviews is a valuable experience for the reader, because she introduces us to the "faces" behind the debates over homosexuality in the Church. We meet parents of gay children, gays in life-long committed relationships, gays who were pastors, and pastors who have been transformed by and transforming in their ministry with gays. These faces remind us that all of the debate about the "homosexual issue" ultimately impacts the lives of real persons, who are our neighbors, our pastors, our relatives--our brothers and sisters in Christ. Beverly Cole challenges the Church to look beyond the abstract debates and into these faces, so that we might respond with the love of Christ.

~Paul Custodio Bube-W.Lewis McColgan Professor of Religion

For anyone who does not have first hand experience or who struggles accepting someone who is gay, Beverly Cole's book is a must. She gives a stirring, sensitive portrayal of a number of men and women whose lives were turned upside down upon their own acceptance of who they were. The interviews highlight the importance and gift of each person who shares his or her thoughts and feelings. Their struggles are monumental and oftentimes heroic. Finding God seemed impossible, but they persevered with and sometimes without the support of family. We very clearly see the importance of God's creation in this book.

~Dr. Carmen Chirveno-author of *Daughter of the Spirit: A Soul's Journey Home*

These accounts of faithful spirit-filled United Methodists bring us face-to-face to encounter God in the midst of courageous vulnerability. Such face-to-face encounters are recorded on the pages of Voices from the Kingdom: All God's Children Have Keys. *These interviews reveal that God is already at work making all things new--right here in the United Methodist Church--right now.*

~Troy Plummer-Executive Director of the Reconciling Ministries Network of the United Methodist Church

How does Beverly Cole know these voices are from the Kingdom of God? It's not all that hard to tell. These are quiet testimonies of peace and harmony experienced in hopelessness. Yet, there is hope in every story found only in resurrection. Don't weep for these sons and daughters who know God's joy. Weep for a society that offers them rejection. The Christian faith is in these voices. Listen up!

~Reverend William Salmon

Voices from the Kingdom *is an absolute truth. Beverly has interviewed a diverse group of the faithful, both gay and straight and has elicited stories of our gay children, friends and loved ones sitting in the pews feeling misunderstood, undervalued, and yes, even fearful because of their sexual orientation. It gives insight into the blessing it is to them when they find a place of love and concern that is eager to use the gifts that God has given them. It also tells of many who have come to a greater understanding who see the truth that gay and lesbian Christians have a spirituality that is so valuable because of the hardships they have had to endure. Members of all denominations must put aside negative conventional wisdom and old religious ideologies about homosexuality and not exclude our gay and lesbian children from worship and service.*

~Beverly Barbo-Author of *The Walking Wounded*

Defending the sins of stigmatization reflects a losing battle. Those who sought to justify apartheid in South Africa, or racism and segregation in America, ultimately experienced defeat and shame. Inclusiveness ultimately triumphs over exclusiveness because God's love is for all people. Beverly Cole's Voices from the Kingdom *challenges the Church to repent and return to the heart of the Gospel by affirming and including gay and lesbian persons at all levels in the church and society.*

~Donald E. Messer-President and Professor Emeritus, Iliff School of Theology, Executive Director, Center for the Church and Global AIDS

To Jesus because of whom he ate with

PREFACE

"What does the Lord require of you
but to do justice,
and to love kindness,
and to walk humbly with your God?"

Jesus is my hero. The way he lived his life is an inspiration to me. Story after story from the Gospels acquaints me with a man who never hesitated to share a meal with the most ordinary of persons. He was comfortable with the poor, the sick, and those whose hands were rough and scarred from a lifetime of labor. Scoundrel or outcast, man or woman, the elderly or children--Jesus ate with them all. The kind of people with whom you shared table fellowship drew society's attention in Jesus' time.

Even in this era of individualism, who a person chooses to call friend and associate can quickly color his or her reputation. It was no different in the communities where Jesus walked, taught, preached and healed. Yet, he chose the most unlikely members of society with whom to surround himself. They were a diverse lot--women, fishermen, a tax collector, a physician, a doubter, a man weak in character and even a traitor. Although he found himself frustrated with them at times, he trusted that they could be tutored and groomed to carry on his work and offer God's message to the world after he was gone. One of his lessons I value the most is that compassion and tending the needs of people takes precedent over religious law. He taught it in the parables and he demonstrated it over and over in his relationships with people.

The well from which Jesus drew compassion seemed to be bottomless. He had a heart that was always open to those who were in need. His love wasn't reserved exclusively for those who looked, thought, or acted the way he did. He saw right through whatever walls of protection people hid behind, seeing directly into their hearts. When people were hurting, he was hurting with them, and he always addressed that hurt with unconditional love, especially to the poor and the outcasts. Christians are called to emulate his life as best they can.

I love the United Methodist Church. It was under its roof that I met this man, Jesus. It was within the walls of that institution that I learned about his love for all people. It was in the youth choir that I sang praises to God in community worship. Youth group in high school provided a space for me to grow, learn, have fellowship and attend church camp. My parents were Methodist Youth Fellowship sponsors, so it was a family endeavor. The community I valued and trusted as a youth has carried over into my adult life. My faith, sustained partly by my church, is paramount to my existence.

Recently, I read a book by Phillip Gulley and James Mulholland, titled *If God is Love: Rediscovering Grace in an Ungracious World*. In its pages I ran across this quotation by Tony Campolo: "To be full of the Spirit is to have your heart broken by the things that break the heart of God."

In the very depths of my soul, I feel that the Church is breaking the heart of God with its bickering and fighting over homosexuality--over making the decision as to whether or not to allow homosexual people full participation in that institution. I know it's breaking my heart, but my grief is minor compared to the hurt that has been inflicted on the gay community through this conflict. Many have given up and left the Church. Others are optimistic and keep holding onto hope, trying to remain anonymous in the pews, participating wherever they are allowed. A few are angry. In the midst of all of this, the Church is missing a wonderful opportunity to practice the love of Jesus while benefiting from the gifts and graces that gay Christians can bring to the faith community's table.

Thich Nhat Hahn is a Buddhist monk who was close friends with Thomas Merton, a well-known Trappist monk and mystic in the Catholic tradition. They recognized each other as brothers. They had enormous respect for each other's faith traditions and together they had hoped to bring Eastern and Western religions into harmony with each other. Unfortunately, Merton died in an accident before they could realize their dream. In the following quotation from *Be Still and Know: Reflections from Living Buddha, Living Christ*, Thich Nhat Hanh addresses the concept of the Kingdom of God.

The place to touch the Kingdom of God is within us. We do not have to die to arrive at the gate of Heaven. In fact, we have to be truly alive. If we touch life deeply enough, the Kingdom of God will become a reality here and now. This is not a matter of devotion. It is a matter of practice.

Thich Nhat Hanh, in many of his books, writes about touching and watering the wholesome seeds in ourselves. He says that in this practice we touch the seeds of understanding and loving-kindness in ourselves which, in turn, benefits our own happiness and ultimately, the happiness of others. I find this idea compelling.

At a Lenten service in my local church several years ago, a United Methodist pastor set forth a similar idea. His name was George, and he talked about the tradition of "the cross and the flame"--a United Methodist symbol. He specifically focused on the flame, saying that none of us is able to participate in all the ministries of the church. "Each person in the Church must find his or her passion," he said, "and then we have to fan each other's flames." What he was referring to was fellow Christians supporting and encouraging each other in the areas of ministry that they found exciting and meaningful. That's what brings the Kingdom to fruition.

When we, as the Church, tell the gay community that their experiences of self aren't good enough and their stories of faith don't matter--we trample their seeds into the dust and throw water on their flames. But if we listen to who they are, what they know to be true in their faith journeys, and treat their experiences of the Kingdom with respect and value, we all win.

What follows in the pages of *Voices from the Kingdom: All God's Children Have Keys* is documentation of the effect this controversy has had on individual lives and faith journeys.

The fourteen interviews, conducted over a year's time, document the hope and the heartache that the issue of homosexuality and the Church has brought into the lives of so many. The gay and lesbian Christians, their families, their pastors, and their bishops open up their lives, allowing us to walk along with them on their faith journeys as they find water to irrigate their seeds and oxygen to keep their flames burning. Numerous times this takes place in unlikely circumstances and in spite of the obstacles set before them by the institution. Some did not feel comfortable using their real names, but they still wanted to participate. Their requests for anonymity have been honored.

In the opening interview, Pastor Nick recounts how he took a stand against the status quo in his community of pastors by openly disagreeing with their public statement that they must "love the sinner but hate the sin." His "liberal serving of mashed potatoes" philosophy on faith comes back to support him in an unexpected way.

Sue loved the Flannigans, her choir directors at church, from the time she was little until she was in the eleventh grade, and they loved her. As Sue shares the story of "the ring," we understand what real, unconditional love is. Love shows itself over and over in this story, and there's little doubt that it influenced Sue's call into her life's work.

Ruth tells of her frustration trying to honor her vows while serving as a single, in-the-closet, ordained minister. When taking a leave of absence from the local church pulpit, she found Naomi, the love of her life. Now she enjoys her life with Naomi but must choose between that life and a call to the ministry that she can't ignore.

Fritz and Etta Mae are a gentle and courageous couple who share their story of losing two sons within nine months of each other to AIDS. Even in the midst of church politics, this bishop and his wife stood strong in their ministry to educate about AIDS and bring grace and compassion to those suffering from the disease, and their families.

An appreciation of diversity is a trait shared by families who embrace their gay and lesbian sons and daughters, as well as their friends. Jerry and Maudell describe their journey toward that appreciation, and tell how it beckoned them into a life of activism in their retirement.

God provides for our deepest needs, but sometimes it takes a while. Chuck, a married, ordained United Methodist minister struggled for years with being gay and Christian, while serving as a popular and effective clergyman in his appointed congregations. It took a trip to New Mexico and a conversation with a young artist from Paris to open Chuck's heart so that he could love himself. The artist's story of irony turned into a holy moment.

Brian W. knew about church. He'd been active all his life and could mix it up with the best of his challengers, but the greatest gift he ever received was from an American Baptist by the name of Roger Williams, who introduced him to "soul liberty."

Bishop Wilke had loved the Bible his whole life. He and his wife wrote the Disciple Bible Study, which has inspired and educated Christians around the world. He takes on the difficult task of talking about the troublesome scriptures used to exclude homosexuals from acceptance in church and society.

Our son, Eric, and his partner are the only two in this book who don't attend a United Methodist Church. Joe is an ordained Metropolitan Community Church pastor and Eric is an active member of that church. The MCC is a church that was originally established for the gay and lesbian community because so many of them had no place to worship. Joe and Eric love the fact that they met at church while volunteering for a program that provides hot meals for the homeless in San Francisco. Within the walls of that MCC Church, Joe realized his call to ministry. At that church's altar, Joe and Eric pledged their lives to each other. In their life together, being gay and Christian is celebrated.

No one thinks much further than what to wear when having their photo taken for the church directory, but Kate and Sara were in a quandary as to whether or not to have their picture taken as a family with their daughter, Faith, or separately. The fuss they were unable to avoid ultimately provided a justice opportunity for everyone involved.

And then there is the story of Brian S., a youth coordinator who is gay. At the time of our interview, he had just participated in a national church conference where the delegates voted to tighten the restrictions on homosexual participation in the church he loves. That exclusion sent him into despair. An ex-con who was trying to keep from relapsing into drug use was the unlikely stranger who unexpectedly reassured Brian of God's presence in his life.

Bruce and Virginia, both ordained pastors, have a passion for justice work. Little did they know how their experiences in the Civil Rights Movement of the 'sixties would prepare them for dealing with having a gay son.

Individual Christians have different ways of expressing their faith. Doug and Chris have always done it through their love of music. In their interview, they share their very different experiences of being gay teens associated with church during their youth. The diverse congregation that actively embraces them in their adulthood allows them to use music to give glory to God.

In the final interview Reverend Dell describes his experience when he came into conflict with the Church. He knew then how Jesus must have felt about the law and, like Jesus, Reverend Dell chose the way of compassion. He shares with us his "ministry in the loopholes," the creative way he has found to stay and minister within the system.

All that God requires of us is that we take the journey using the keys we are given to unlock the doors along the way. The flame of justice burns bright behind one door. The seeds of kindness bear fruit as we pass through another. Each child of God has been sent to find his or her way through the Kingdom of God, but all of God's children have keys.

Acknowledgements

Our family used to check in on an elderly lady named Mrs. Stoltzman. Whenever we would take her someplace or do something nice for her she would always say, "Thanks is such a small word with such a big meaning." Gratitude is another word like thanks. When we have a great deal to be grateful for, life is especially good.

I am extremely grateful for my United Methodist congregation--my church family. It is with them that I can study and grow in faith, find and give support in times of need, and with whom I can try on my social justice hat when talking about the issue of homosexuality. They have been willing to stretch and grow toward truly living into the denomination's slogan "Open Hearts, Open Minds, Open Doors." I have always had pastoral support as well. It's because of that love and support that I have been able to share our personal story beyond my church's doors. Not all Christian families with gay children enjoy that privilege.

It takes more than faith community support to get a book on the bookshelves, however. Patricia Traxler has been a friend for a number of years and my faithful editor when I have needed professional help with my writing. Her experience, expertise and insights have been abundantly helpful through my writing process.

Nick Warner has also been tremendously helpful as he edited each chapter with both English major and pastoral credentials. Thanks to Marilyn Ericson and Bill and Beverly Salmon for helping with editing, as well.

The easiest part of doing this book was the writing. Hearing the faith stories of all those I interviewed was fascinating and inspiring. You'll share in that experience as you read their accounts. So, thank you Nick, Sue, Ruth and Naomi, Fritz and Etta Mae, Jerry and Maudell, Chuck, Brian W., Bishop Wilke, Joe and Eric, Kate and Sara, Brian S. Bruce and Virginia, Doug and Chris, and Rev. Dell. You have made a difference.

The most difficult part of getting this book out was wrestling with the computer. I am strongly intuitive and that doesn't work with computers. Keith Holmes rescued me a number of times, helping me get this body of work into a publishable form.

Derius Mammen and Vanessa, Jostens Printing and Publishing, were invaluable in getting *Voices from the Kingdom* into print.

Family is another word like thanks--it isn't big enough to cover the subject. There was a section of gay/lesbian interviews that was a part of the manuscript of my first book, *Cleaning Closets: A Mother's Story*. It was omitted from the final publication. My mom said reading them had been very helpful to her in finding understanding, thus the inspiration for this collection of interviews.

When I talk about whether being gay is a choice or not, I always say, "You don't choose to be gay, but you can choose how to be gay, just like you can choose how to be straight." I am pleased with how our son, Eric, has chosen to live his life as a gay person. He is a hard worker, kind, and thoughtful. He has chosen a partner, Joe, who has the same great character traits. Family and faith are very important to them and we love them both.

I am pleased with how our daughter, Traci, has chosen to live her life as a straight person. She is a hard worker, is kind and thoughtful and a person of faith. Family is very important to her. We love her and appreciate her support, both for us and Eric and Joe.
My husband, Dale is my ongoing supporter and encourager and I am grateful to have him in my life.

TABLE OF CONTENTS

FOREWORD

When I began teaching in a theological school in the late sixties, I had no "position" on homosexuality. I had never considered it seriously. I suppose I thought about such things in a way that was not distant from that of the official position of the United Methodist Church today. Up to that time I only knew that I knew two gay men in my life, and no lesbians. When I arrived at my teaching position in the seminary, however, I found a curriculum that attempted to put students in as many different situations with as many different people as possible. These became key ingredients for our theological reflection and for reflections on implications for ministry.

My first connections with the gay and lesbian community introduced me to a new world. Invitations to gay balls, to meetings of gay action groups, and to gay and lesbian bars were well beyond anything I had ever known. What became even more important was contact with and ongoing friendships with gay and lesbian people who were devout Christians and members of the church. Hearing their stories, their love of Christ, and their devotion to the church opened my eyes and my heart to a range of experiences and to the lives of people I did not know even existed. I learned about myself, as I would later learn about others, that the most effective way to change hearts and minds about homosexuality is to engage people in new experiences and new relationships with gay and lesbian people. I simply could not deny the love of Christ and the church that I found among gay and lesbian Christians.

Somewhere in these days I began to meet gay and lesbian people who were married, and I refuse to place quotes on the word marriage. They were married in the most faithful sense of that word. Their commitment to each other, their devotion to marriage in a fully Christian sense became undeniably clear to me. I found it impossible to think otherwise. I also ran into parents and other kin who had fought through all the prejudice and the discounting of their gay and lesbian family members. I was simply moved by their witness in the face of the hurt, the struggle, the courage, and, strangely, the faithfulness of these very people to the church that had so often excluded their loved ones and, sometimes, them as well.

Of course, I studied the biblical passages, having done that now for nearly forty years. That handful of passages simply cannot sustain the kind of absolute against gay and lesbian practice that conservatives and even the United Methodist Church claim. In fact, there is growing evidence that conservatives know this. It can be seen in their increasing focus on "the complementarity of the sexes" and their increasing emphasis here. The plain fact is that they are losing this battle, hence the reason why they become more rigid, more given to legalism in the church, and heavier handed.

But this issue of homosexuality will not finally be solved by greater clarity about the few allusions and references to same-sex practices in the Bible, or by desperate claims about the "ontology of the sexes." Rather it will come from the church and others meeting faithful Christian people who are gay and lesbian. It will come from hearing their stories and seeing the work of the Holy Spirit in their lives, in their marriages, in their devotion to Christ, and in their faithfulness to the church.

This is so clearly what Beverly Cole is doing in this book. One finds here stories of gay and lesbian people and also their parents, friends, kin, and loved ones. Here there are clergy, bishops, and laity telling their stories and how and why they changed not only their views but their very lives and the shape of their witness. They could no longer hold to the prohibitive stance of the church on homosexuality which stood in such discontinuity with not just their experience, but the central claims of their faith.

The testimonies here are those of courage, to be sure, but they are so very much more than that. They are proclamations of faithfulness. How do people not only go on, but become people of hope in the face of the death of one's children or loved ones to AIDS? How does one remain committed to a church that blocks one's call to ministry? How can a homosexual couple devoted to each other in Christian marriage remain devoted to a church that denies a marital relationship of love and faithfulness that they see as intrinsic to the Christian faith itself? These are only a few of the questions addressed here in narrative form. This book is a testament to the faith, a witness to a horizon of hope. We are not only blessed by these stories. We are made stronger by them, and we are prepared for a new thing God is doing in the church and in the world.

Tex Sample

INTRODUCTION

"We are living in a very painful period. The Church always moves forward through crisis. Crises are times when cracks appear in the Church, through which the Holy Spirit pours."

This comment came at the conclusion of a BBC documentary, *Queer and Catholic*. The documentary is a young British priest's story of struggle with his deep Catholic faith as it conflicts with the doctrines of the Catholic Church. His anxiety came from the fact that he is a gay man attempting to sort out and make sense of what he feels in his heart, while the Catholic Church tells him his homosexuality is sinful.

I met Mark and the other members of his film crew when I was in San Francisco attending the holy union/marriage of my son, Eric, and his partner, Joe. The crew's presence, although a bit disruptive, was welcomed--they were filming Eric and Joe's ceremony as a part of the documentary they were doing. This segment would deal with the Catholic Church's stance against gay relationships and same-sex marriage.

After we had become acquainted, Mark shared with me the story of how he was "outed" to his family in England. He described how he had kept his feelings of attraction for males to himself, thinking he was keeping this aspect of himself a secret from his family. One morning at breakfast, his mother asked him if he was gay. Startled, he asked her where she'd gotten that idea. She told him he had been calling out a man's name in his sleep. It was then, although with some relief, that he'd had to face the reality that he was indeed gay.

His story put me in the kitchen of a person of a different culture than my own American culture--a person whose family practiced a faith different from my own Protestant faith and yet, we had a significant thing in common. Mark was a gay person of faith who loved the Church, and loved the figure of Jesus he had grown up with. I was the mother of a gay son and a person of faith who felt the Church needed to look at the issue of homosexuality with new eyes. From my point of view, the Church's policies excluding full participation of gays and lesbians in the life of the Church were in conflict with the principles set forth by the Jesus I had come to know and love. Mark and I had similar stories in this area. In our conversation I affirmed who he was as a gay man and a Christian, and encouraged him to keep nudging the Church toward positive change in their policies regarding gays.

Perhaps like the Church, I need nudging in my life to open the cracks in my resistance to the Holy Spirit so transformation can take place. I have felt a heightened awareness of that Spirit working in my life the last fifteen years or so. The nudging was especially apparent in an incident when I was in my late forties.

I had enrolled in a class offered through the University of Minnesota--Split Rock Arts Program in Duluth, Minnesota. The emphasis of the class was on gaining the tools needed to keep a journal of your daily life. Each day we would have journal writing assignments to complete and read in class. One day the assignment was to write a journal entry on sexuality. I was far from home in a class with people I didn't know very well and would probably never see again, so I mustered up my courage and wrote that I'd needed to change my opinion of what "normal" sexuality was when I realized I had a son who was gay. At my personal conference the next day with Phoebe, the instructor, I was startled by the challenge she dropped in my lap. Phoebe suggested that I share our family story in book form to be made available to other families who were personally struggling with the issue of homosexuality--especially Christian families. I thought she was crazy!

However, Phoebe's challenge kept eating at me. I wrestled for a number of months with the idea, but continually tried to talk myself out of actually writing the book. First of all, I didn't have much writing experience. Secondly, I didn't "do" controversy. I also kept asking myself why in the world I would want to put our family's personal, intimate story on the bookshelves of strangers! My arguments didn't hold up. Every time I would try to back away from Phoebe's challenge, something would happen that would convince me to follow through with the project.

Finally, with the support and encouragement of family, friends, and therapists who were friends, *Cleaning Closets: A Mother's Story* was written and published. I believe the Holy Spirit was right in the middle of the whole process.

Cleaning Closets seemed to do what it was intended to do. In the past twelve years, I have heard from numerous gay men and lesbians who have found that sharing our story with their families has helped them to deal with having a gay family member. The response from the gay community and their families has been very rewarding.

Shortly after *Cleaning Closets* was published, I had a visit with David Polk, the Chalice Press editor who had worked with me throughout the publishing process. I asked him what he thought about my writing another book. He asked me if I thought I had another book in me. At the time I wasn't sure what the subject of another book might be, so I dismissed the thought.

A number of years later on the third of July, I was driving out of town to bring my mother to our home for a holiday visit. I was adjusting to a new car, and I strayed into the oncoming traffic lane while trying to adjust my cruise control. Luckily, I missed the family van that was coming toward me in that lane, but in overcorrecting I ended up in the ditch with a deep cut under my eye that required five stitches. There were no other injuries, but my car was totaled.

In the weeks that followed, when friends would tell me how lucky I was, I would casually reply that I must have more work to do on this earth. A few weeks after the accident I received a call from Jerry Longwell, the brother of a woman who has been a member of my local congregation for years. He was the Jurisdictional Coordinator of the Reconciling Parents' Network, a part of the Reconciling Ministries Network in the United Methodist Church, and he had a son who was gay. He asked me if I would serve as Reconciling Parents' Network Coordinator in my Annual Conference. I immediately thought of my "more work to do" comment and said, "Sure."

A few months later, at a Jurisdictional meeting in Dallas, we were trying to come up with ideas that would facilitate understanding and encourage change in the Church's resistance to full inclusion of gays and lesbians. As we sat around the table exchanging stories, I realized I did have another book in me, and it was time for it to be written. There was that Holy Spirit again, dusting off the keys of my computer. In the original manuscript of *Cleaning Closets*, there had been a section of interviews with people from the gay community who were willing to share their personal stories. After my mother had read the manuscript, she commented that she'd found the interviews to be the most interesting section of the book and the most helpful for her understanding of gays and lesbians as real people. Ultimately, the interviews were not printed as part of the final book, but the idea of putting together a collection of interviews had always been in the back of my mind. Maybe it was time to get started.

I found that idea validated in the pages of a book entitled *Turning to One Another: Simple Conversations to Restore Hope in the Future*, by Margaret J. Wheatley. This paragraph from the book was especially meaningful to me:

I love the biblical passage: "Whenever two or more are gathered, I am there." It describes for me the holiness of moments of real listening. The health, wholeness, holiness of a new relationship forming. I have a T-shirt from one conference that reads: "You can't hate someone whose story you know." You don't have to like the story, or even the person telling you their story. But listening creates a relationship. We move closer to one another.

The stories in this book are the faith stories of gay men and lesbian women who have found a way to honor that which is holy in their lives, in spite of the Church's resistance to accepting them as they are. These are the stories of clergy whose personal and spiritual lives have been changed forever because of their experiences with gay parishioners and their families. These are the stories of Christian parents who, because they have a gay child, have come to enjoy the blessings of diversity in their lives and faith journeys. Although the majority of these interviews are from people who are United Methodists, the struggle depicted here continues in nearly every mainstream Christian denomination in existence, and the stories will resonate with people of every faith. It is my hope that these interviews will create the cracks through which the Holy Spirit can flow into the Church and that the people who have shared their spiritual journeys will be the catalyst for change--transforming the Church into a place of love and tolerance--a place where everyone will be welcome to sit at God's bountiful table.

Nick

Mashed Potatoes Theology

Nick has been a huge part of my journey toward salvation and wholeness. For eight wonderful years, he pastored Trinity United Methodist Church where I presently attend. His shared keen intellect and his store of "wise" sayings are still tucked away in our hearts and we pull them out from time to time as needed. One of those for me is "We don't go to church for fire insurance."

My husband, Dale, has another memory of Nick's clever wit used to make a point. Nick was new to Trinity, and a group of members met with him to share our goals for the future of the church. We were given the assignment of drawing a picture that would illustrate what church was for us. Nick was to do this, also. When the discussion made its way around the circle to Nick, he held up his drawing for all to see. On the page were two simple images, a shepherd's staff and a fishhook. When he was asked to explain, he made a typical "Nick" comment. "By hook or by crook, we're going to make Trinity United Methodist Church grow." And grow it did.

Members of the congregation felt safe with Nick. He had a genuine interest in each and every member of the flock. His typical greeting was, "How you doing? How's the family?" When he served communion along the altar railing, he called each congregant by name as he served them. It made the sacrament spiritually personal.

Nick's sermons challenged us to think. His words inspired us to committed personal growth and an expanded capacity to love others. We never felt even a small hint of judgment in his words from the pulpit.

Nick had visited with our son, Eric on several occasions about the possibility of Eric's becoming a minister. He recognized a spirit in Eric that he felt would lend itself well to that calling. He teased Eric, telling him that his training in theater would be helpful in speaking from the pulpit. "A good preacher can be more effective with a sense of theatrics in his or her style."

The sum total of who Nick was-- intelligent, funny, trustworthy, non-judgmental,

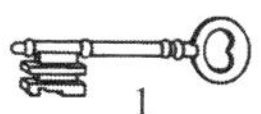

and sincerely interested in each person's welfare--gave me the courage to go into his office for some help and support when I needed it most.

It was a few days after Christmas in 1985 when I pulled into the parking lot of the church where I had been active for almost fifteen years. I was hurting, scared, and in mourning. I needed support through a personal crisis and I was feeling alone with my pain. I had just found out our son, Eric was gay and I didn't think I could tell anyone in my congregation, my church family, what I was going through. Eric was still in high school and needed his privacy as he struggled with what his homosexuality meant for him. Thank God I could talk to Nick.

I was welcomed into his office with a typical friendly greeting, in which he inquired about me and about my family. He had opened the door for a difficult conversation.

My soul was laid bare, accompanied by a burst of involuntary tears, as I revealed that Eric would not be pursuing a vocation in the ministry. Homosexuals could not be ordained in the United Methodist Church. I told him Eric was gay.

Nick's response was immediate, compassionate, and accompanied by a handful of tissues, along with these words: "It's okay, Beverly. It's thought that about ten percent of the population is homosexual. For ten percent, that's normal. Eric's being gay wasn't caused by anything you or Dale did. He's the same great person he was before you knew. You just know one more thing about him than you did before. Love him like he is. Don't try to change him."

I left Nick's office with a huge burden lifted off my shoulders and the will to deal with whatever this situation would bring. I had hope that everything would be all right. Eventually, I wrote about our life-changing session in a book entitled, Cleaning Closets: A Mothers Story. *Our original time together had put me on the right path to do many things I would never have guessed I'd do.*

Twenty years later, Nick was pastoring another United Methodist Church that was both considerably larger in numbers and budget than our church and interestingly, was named Trinity. We had remained friends over the years. I had decided to write this book, and Nick's faith story fit right into it. I went to see him in his church office to do an interview.

Let's start with your growing up time. What was your experience growing up in the church?

Nick: I grew up in a small Methodist church. It wasn't "United" then. If we had twenty on a Sunday, that was a big Sunday. I always had a role there. I remember separating out Sunday school papers and taking them around to the different classes for that Sunday. By junior high I got to read the Scripture sometimes, so I was always included in what was going on there.

My call to ministry really happened there, as I looked at student pastors who drove fifteen miles from a nearby college to be in our pulpit and to serve us. I liked who they were, and I liked the idea of preaching on Sunday. My relationship with them sort of opened up the possibility of an occupational choice that eventually turned into a deeper calling. We were there every Sunday. I grew up on a farm, and my dad never cut wheat on Sunday morning. You went to church and stayed for the covered dish if there was one. If there was a church meeting through the week, I was there.

Was your calling a gradual one or did you have a specific experience that told you that this was where God wanted you to be?

I guess it was gradual. I liked what I heard about the "Good News," and I felt like I wanted to share that with people. I was challenged on an intellectual level by a couple of professors in college, Wallace Gray and Andy Key. They got me to thinking about the faith and especially biblical literature. It all kind of solidified my junior and senior years of college when I was asked by the District Superintendent to come be one of those student pastors in two small town churches. Jim Reed, who was a great role model, supervised me. In the midst of all that, I discovered that I had some gifts and graces. I enjoyed the preaching and making calls. Jim's support encouraged me, too.

Tell me where you went to seminary.

I went to Union Theological Seminary in New York City, a very progressive place. I grew in my love of biblical languages there.

Has your philosophy or theology stayed about the same or have you changed over the years?

I've remained pretty much mainstream over the years, having been exposed to some great Old Testament scholarship tools by Dr. Key. I love the word "liberal" because it tends to mean more. If you have a liberal helping of mashed potatoes, you get more. So I feel that in the terms of faith, being liberal in beliefs gives you more, not less. I've actually built on that.

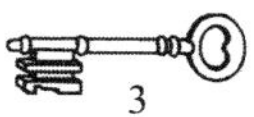

Do you remember telling me once that if a person was becoming more exclusive in his or her thinking, he or she wasn't growing in faith? On the other hand, those people who were becoming more inclusive were growing.

I think the biblical journey is one that goes from exclusion to inclusion. The Old Testament starts out with a very limited scope regarding who the covenant people were. It's almost a geographical God. Add to that the unending laws for daily living, often connected with ritual unseemliness, and it's a very restrictive lifestyle for God's people.

As you move through the Biblical story it becomes all-inclusive. Walls get broken down. Jesus breaks rules right and left. There are stories of Jesus' touching lepers, definitely violating the cleanliness code. His conversation with the Samaritan woman at the well was a double taboo, speaking to a Samaritan and a woman. Jesus cleared the crowd that was ready to stone a woman caught in adultery by asking them who among them was without sin. No one could throw the first stone, even though biblical law prescribed her punishment.

The original Christian movement was really a reformed Jewish movement of those who believed in Jesus. By the middle of Acts, the old standards begin to fall away.

So we've always had trouble with change.

Sure. Early believers had to take a look at the old laws and attitudes. They had to decide which laws they were going to hold on to and which ones they would let go of.

In the middle of the book of Acts, Chapter 15, the early Christians dropped two of the big ones--male circumcision would no longer be required of those wanting to be part of the faith community, and the laws connected with "ritually unclean foods" were no longer binding.

I love the story of Peter being on the roof of a friend's house and having the vision of a sheet dropping down from God, full of religiously forbidden foods. God says it's okay to eat these foods, and Peter doesn't know what to think. Not eating those foods had been a longstanding requirement in Jewish law. God is full of surprises.

Yes, and another good one is Philip's baptizing the Ethiopian eunuch in chapter eight of Acts.

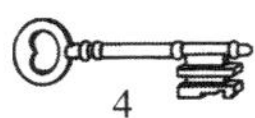

This presents two of the problems, right off the bat, that the contemporary church is dealing with--someone who is of a different race and also sexually different. The question the Ethiopian eunuch asked-- "What is to prevent me from being baptized?"-- still rings true today.

So what do we need to learn from this? Are there things we need to let go of as a faith community? Are there things we need to look at through a different lens? Maybe homosexuality is one of those issues.

This is the reality of what happens within the institutional church. When certain statements are made or stands taken, there is a price to pay. Certain people will be lost. That's not new, however. The Methodist Church was split another time in our history over the issue of slavery. There were passages in the Bible that could be interpreted to support slavery and some people did that. There were others in the church who saw slavery as oppressive and so there was a split. Even at that, from 1939 until 1968 there was what was known as the Central Jurisdiction--a structure by which the denomination was largely segregated. It existed until the Methodist Church and the Evangelical United Brethren denominations merged in 1968 to form the United Methodist Church.

Do you think the fact that the homosexual population is estimated at from four to ten percent of the whole is part of the problem of resistance in the church today? Do people feel that such a small number of people aren't worth all the fuss?

Well, some certainly appear to! At that juncture it really becomes a question of "What does it mean to be the Church?" What we really have here is an opportunity to be the Church with a capital "C."

Some want to say it's only four percent. But when you look at what it really means to be the Church of Christ, that argument evaporates.

You have mentioned the price a church pays when pastors take a stand on controversial issues. Share the story of how that played out in your congregation.

Let's just do a brief history of my involvement in this congregation. I've been here seventeen years. That would explain a few gray hairs. The first four years you might call culture shock, getting adjusted to a new congregation that was

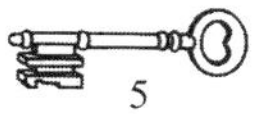

cautious about making the changes it would take to grow. Those changes did take place and we were off and running.

The next eight years were great. We were growing in numbers and finances, adding more services on Sunday mornings and additional worthwhile programming. We were in a good place. We had a relationship of trust.

In 2002, I was blessed with this new associate, Amy, fresh out of seminary. She was extremely bright, gifted and hard working. We were having a great time together, and then this article appeared in the local newspaper.

The article appeared on March 6, 2004, stating that "Churches Confront Gay Issue" and the by-line on that was "Hutchinson area pastors say Scripture denounces homosexuality but they're promoting the attitude of 'Love the sinner but hate the sin.'"

Now, it is not Amy's and my style to stir up controversy, but we looked at each other on Monday after that had been in the faith section on Saturday and said, "This just can't stand." This was a statement of where area pastors are, and we weren't there.

So we co-wrote a letter to the editor of the newspaper. It appeared on Monday, March 15th, and that was really the beginning of the journey. Here are some excerpts from that article:

"As two Hutchinson area clergy, we find the slogan, 'Love the sinner, but hate the sin" to be trite, condescending and impossible. As United Methodist clergy, we are indeed a part of a denomination that at the present time does not ordain "self-avowed, practicing homosexuals" or allow ministers to perform same-sex unions. At the last General Conference in 2000 where such issues are defined, the vote was approximately sixty percent to forty percent in support of the current positions.

However, United Methodists are also on record supporting the civil rights of gay and lesbian persons and understand them to be graced and gifted for full participation within the church.

In the past we have discriminated against our fellow human beings on the basis of their skin color, their gender, and their religion. We are now focused on discrimination against others based on whom they love.

People of gay and lesbian orientation sit in the pews of our churches and are important members of our church families. God's Word must never be used in ways that are ungodly or that hurt any of God's children. When Scripture is used for political advantage and as the cover for writing overt discrimination into our legal code, those who take seriously the inclusive love of God must stand in prophetic, albeit unpopular, opposition.

Before we did this, we ran the letter past our Staff Parish Relations Committee, who read it, some with wider eyes than others. We told them that there would be ramifications from this. Although we had previously made clear our stance on gay and lesbian issues from the pulpit, we said there would probably be people who would leave our church over the letter. In reality some church members did leave, and we ended up experiencing a "worship boycott" by about three-dozen members. Overall, average attendance dropped by about twenty and we lost about six percent of pledged giving. Yet there have been some wonderfully positive results. Some others have started attending Trinity because of our compassionate, inclusive stance. Also, several important, substantive pastoral visits have happened with families who have since felt free to share about a gay or lesbian family member.

Would you have been as tuned into this issue had you not been an alternate delegate to General Conference?

Oh, yes. Whether or not I was a delegate to General Conference, we just couldn't let this stand. We have been very disappointed in the clergy's response to this. We heard from several who said they were with us and thanked us for stating our case so well so that they didn't have to. Others have said they could never say anything like that in our local community. They agreed, but just wouldn't make the statement.

I had the opportunity to visit with you after General Conference, at which time you shared that story with me. The term you used for what was happening was that your congregation was bleeding. To use an interesting analogy to that situation, Jesus ended up bleeding because he chose love over the law just as you are doing.

It's interesting you would say that, considering one term used for folks claiming to have a liberal philosophy is "bleeding heart." Jesus was the first bleeding heart, there on the cross!

Lets go ahead and talk about your experience at General Conference.

I did see just a slight movement in a positive direction in the church's thinking. I guess part of that is because we talked more about it at Pittsburgh than we did at Cleveland four years prior, at General Conference. In Cleveland in 2000, the

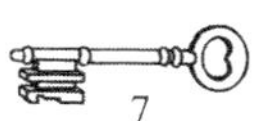

vote was sixty percent to forty percent against changing the Discipline to read, "Although most do not condone the practice of homosexuality and consider it incompatible with some Christian teaching..."

In Pittsburgh, 2004, rather than trying to change the wording in the Discipline that seemed to be so firmly set, the moderating plan was to insert a statement stating, "Faithful Christians disagree as to the compatibility of homosexuality with Christian teaching." Faithful Christians disagree! What an honest statement!

Well, we got a closer vote--fifty-five percent to forty-five percent. Now, this raises two points--we disagree and pretty evenly, as it were. However, politically, and this is a political issue, there was unwillingness for the majority to allow the rest to be called "faithful."

That's really amazing. So, was most of the attention focused on the wording in the Book of Discipline, as far as the homosexual issue was concerned?

There was, in legislative committee at this Conference, kind of an ugliness that wanted to stick the issue of the performance of same-sex unions with being a chargeable offense. It was a highly charged issue. My recollection is that it passed by only ten votes. 445 to 455, or something like that. There was even some question about its being all right to celebrate a couple being together for a long time but not celebrating if the relationship was just starting. We were just shaking our heads. We're getting really legalistic here. I was really freed up to minister to gay couples in my congregation when it was pointed out to me that there was a service for the BLESSING OF A HOME in the United Methodist Book of Worship. Using that as a form of celebration of those within a committed same-sex relationship is about as close as we can come right now.

What are your thoughts on gay marriage?

I guess I'm a traditionalist and linguist on the matter of the word "marriage." I hate the fact that it has been politicized. My favorite line that I use when talking about gay marriage, is that if we had found weapons of mass destruction in Iraq we wouldn't even be having this discussion of constitutional amendments. It has ended up being a diversion from other political problems.

Politics aside, if we want linguistically to use that term marriage to refer to male and female, so be it. But, being a humane society, we need to come up with a term or concept, and not just for equal rights and health insurance but equal value for the blessing of the relationship. I'd settle for that. I would hope that the

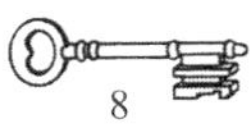

traditionalists could share equal respect for same-sex relationships as for opposite sex relationships. I don't see that it is any threat to the sanctity of marriage. A gay couple across town does not threaten my marriage to Mary Lee.

What we ought to be affirming is the concept of commitment. If you really want to protect the sanctity of marriage, then protect your time with each other and the level of your communication. That goes for both gay and straight couples.

Do you hold out any hope of change in the near future?

There's a new formula for apportioning delegates to General Conference, adopted in 2000, that greatly favors the Southeastern Jurisdiction and the southern part of the South Central Jurisdiction while severely cutting the Western Jurisdiction. That redistributes votes in a way that is not especially promising for change on this issue.

I feel the main hope lies in church-by-church decisions to be in ministry in an open and inclusive way, including its leadership positions. A church's openness within its community tends to be well known. There is a network of knowledge regarding the safer places of worship.

Do you see your congregation ever becoming a "Reconciling Congregation," focused especially on the needs of gay/lesbian congregants?

Our church is not formally titled a "Reconciling Congregation." To adopt formally such a designation can be needlessly divisive. But, because of its present constituency and the public position declared by its pastors, it is recognized as a safe church by reputation, not by its formal designation.

You have an advantage at Trinity, Salina, in that you have Eric and others as "poster children." Having them active in the church as they were growing up put personal faces on the issue. Their families have handled their situations openly and lovingly so that the faith community had a basic starting place for understanding.

Actually, the last thing I want to share with you before we close is an irony in this whole story. The day you came into my office to ask my support for you and your family was the day I started my own journey. Knowing your family helped me personalize the issue of homosexuality and steered me toward a more loving and accepting posture on the issue. It made me look at what the Bible really said in those Scriptures that are misused to condemn homosexuals. I had to get serious about the church really being true to what I have seen as Christ's Church,

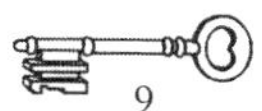

and I had to be willing to speak up for it.

Unbeknownst to me, my journey would prepare me for my own family situation. Our daughter, Ann, has just recently come out to us as a lesbian. I'm embarrassed to say that at first I was afraid that when people found out, they would think my stand on homosexuality was based on that fact. The bottom line, though, is that Ann knows she is fully and unconditionally loved for who she is. Love and acceptance would be my stance, regardless.

This is where your "liberal, overflowing-plateful-of-mashed-potatoes theology of love, grace, and acceptance" speaks for itself. It comes in handy.

I guess it really does. In the meantime, we at Trinity hope that our reputation will further our commitment to being a Christian Church with a Capital "C."

Sue

Dumbest Thing I've Ever Heard

My first contact with Sue was by phone several weeks before the Hearts On Fire Convocation at Lake Junaluska, North Carolina, to be held over Labor Day weekend in the fall of 2005. As Outreach Coordinator for the Reconciling Ministries Network in the United Methodist Church, she was very busy making arrangements and doing all the things there are to do in order to have a successful conference. She was calling to see if I would bring books to the convocation and have a book signing.

I didn't meet her in person until she spoke to us at our pre-convocation Parents Reconciling Network gathering, where she told us a story that deeply touched my heart. I watched Sue live out that week with incredible love and grace under the most stressful of circumstances. Along with just keeping things running smoothly, she had additional pressure outside the gates of the lake facility, thanks to demonstrating Ku Klux Klansmen and opposing religious groups. I made a mental note that I wanted to visit with Sue after the Convocation was over about doing an interview for Voices from the Kingdom.

Several months later, my husband, Dale, and I picked her up at the Reconciling Office in Chicago and took her to lunch. There we talked about her life and her life's work, and decided what to use in the interview. Her passions for her faith, her church, the relationships with those she loves, and her reconciling work became apparent as she shared her life story with me.

What was it like for you, growing up Christian?

Sue: My earliest memory is when we lived with my grandparents for a short time, when I was four and five years old. They took me to Sunday school and I remember the people there being so nice. I learned the "Jesus Loves Me" song. This gave me a real sense of belonging. It was good. When I was in the first grade, our family moved to Erie. We lived downtown near a big, big

Presbyterian church, called Church of the Covenant. We were Presbyterian. Sometimes in an urban church, the kids in the neighborhood aren't the same kids who are at the church. Some people drove in pretty far to be there, but for us it was different because we lived in the neighborhood. The church had a carillon, and at five o'clock we knew to go home to supper by the bells at the church. Everyone went to church in those days, and so we were really beneficiaries of a big program at church. That meant that we had full-time ministers of music, Mr. and Mrs. Flanagan, a married couple. There were so many kids that we had graded choirs.

The Cherub choir was only kindergarten and first grade. The Carol choir was only second and third grade, and they went up from there. By high school we were a choir of forty voices or more. I was also in bell choir once a week, seventh grade through eleventh grade, with Mrs. Flanagan. The scouts met at church, too. By age twelve I had five brothers and two sisters. We were at the church all the time. We had Boy Scouts, Girl Scouts, and at least one of us had choir practice every day of the week. My brother, Bob, and I would take the younger ones to choir. I was probably at that church at least three days a week. I knew everybody in every office. In the summertime Vacation Bible school was two weeks long. In those days, when there were more moms at home, it was easier to find volunteers. By August when the summer was getting boring, we were back in church. When I got older, I took my younger brothers and sisters and stayed the morning, giving out juice and cookies, or whatever I could do.

Church was a huge part of my life. We were a family in which the kids got sent to church rather than going with parents. The consistency of seeing the Flanagans and hearing the stories of Jesus every week of my life from the first grade to the eleventh grade was significant. I can remember being in the first grade, just loving Mrs. Flanagan so much. She had red hair, too, just like me. After Cherub Choir, we would stand in line so she could help us put on our boots and winter clothes when practice was over. Everybody got their minute with Mrs. Flanagan. One week I was in line so she could help me to tie my hat. While I was waiting, and fussing with my hat, I accidentally tied it. I thought, "Oh, no. How am I going to get my minute with Mrs. Flanagan?" I stayed in line until it was my turn, and I just looked up at her and said, "Look, I tied my hat all by myself!" It was worth the wait as she just fussed over my accomplishment.

The Flanagans left for another church before my senior year. I feel so fortunate that I had that consistency. The way they taught and lived their Christianity was permanently imprinted on my understanding and sense of faith. So many young adults say that during their college years they don't go to church. I never went through that phase. I never stopped going to church. I continued to find family there. I often went to the Catholic Church in college, because that is where my friends in the dorm were going. I need to be in church. It's a part of who I am.

At what point during this process did you begin to realize you were a lesbian?

My story is probably like a lot of other people's--you go back in retrospect. I was first attracted to another girl, more than just a friend, when I was in high school. Then in college, that attraction continued on, but I still didn't know I was gay. Now, I think that sounds really ridiculous. It was the early to mid-seventies, and one just never heard about it. If you did hear anything, it was really like kind of a shadow conversation, and I was rarely in shadow conversations. Meanwhile, I felt like I was in love with a woman, and totally isolated. I still did not know I was gay. I did have a relationship in college. We didn't know any other gay people. We were totally isolated. When that was broken off, I had no one to tell. I graduated and began teaching high school in a small town. A friend took a chance and came out to me. Slowly I realized that I knew lots of gay people and I began to realize what might be going on.

As it was revealed, the ones I knew had been afraid to approach me even as friends, and include me in things, partly because I was a Christian--that whole church tension for the gay community. The church kept me isolated, even from the gay community.

I did finally tell a straight friend who was an active Christian, and she thought homosexuality was a sin. I did go through a serious phase of trying not to be gay. It wasn't that hard at first. I was single anyway. I hadn't suffered huge temptations in other things, so I just decided, "If it is wrong, then don't do it." This was when I joined the Edinboro United Methodist Church in 1981. What Campus Crusade groups or fundamentalist Christian groups say to do is find a good church, go, and get involved. That's what I did. I found a church where they remembered my name when I came back the second time. I got involved with the choir and a Bible study, and was there all the time. I enjoyed church. I had community and that was important. Although I had this one friend who knew I was gay and fighting against it, I went through this struggle over my sexuality primarily by myself. This is when you pray the prayers, you do everything in good faith, and you notice nothing has changed.

I think I always knew. Even in the fifth grade, when I remember my girlfriends talking about coming down our long church aisle in their wedding dresses, I

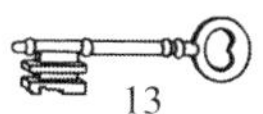

never participated in those conversations. It wasn't the dress. I wore a dress every day to school. I don't think there has ever been a moment in my life when I thought I would be married to a man. I didn't ever feel bad about it. I just knew it was true. So, in my twenties I could admit that I was never going to be heterosexual, but I still wanted to be Christian.

Another thing that fundamentalists said to do was read the Bible. That was good advice, for this was my salvation. I had the Bible open on my kitchen table and I would read a little every day. I joined a Bible study. We were doing the book of Matthew at Edinboro United Methodist Church in the fall of '82. Somewhere I had heard the phrase "Love the sinner and hate the sin" applied to gay people. I am not sure where I picked this up. It was not from my own church or upbringing. That attitude convinced me to try to hate being homosexual.

The problem was that when you start reading the Gospels, the stories of Jesus, and you've been to Sunday school and you knew the Flanagans, it's impossible to hate yourself. I had been afraid that when I turned each page of scripture I would find the place where it said, "You can't be gay!" It's not there. What is there are more and more stories about how God loves us and we're to love our neighbor. That's what pulled me up. That's what started to create a new tension. I'm active in church, I'm praying not to be gay and doing all the things good Christians are supposed to do, but these stories of Jesus are telling me I'm loved and I belong.

About this time, one of my good friends who was gay and had grown up Catholic asked me, "How's it going, not being gay and being Christian?" I said to her, "It's going really well, I'm doing things at church, I'm going to Bible study. I love belonging to this church. The people are really nice," Then I said, "There's just one problem--there's this woman in our Bible study that I really like!"

This is the place where we need to talk about Julie.

Julie was in the Bible study. We both just loved the Bible study so much. I lived right by the church and she lived two blocks away. I would walk her home and we'd just talk about what we were doing in the Gospel of Matthew. Julie did not know that I was gay. I was not quite admitting that that was what the situation was regardless how much I prayed. My friend, the Christian, who was trying to help me not be gay started to panic, because she could tell something had changed.

Julie and I had a lot in common. We both had grown up in church. We both went to church on our own, not because our parents went. We both had experienced a sense of loneliness and yet being ministered to by youth directors and people at church. We both loved talking about the Bible study. Sometimes we would walk back and forth between our houses so we did not have to say goodbye. That fall we went to the college homecoming parade together. Julie didn't know I was gay and I was still in denial, but we really connected that day as friends. In retrospect we count that as our first date and celebrate our anniversary every year on Homecoming.

When did you both discover that your relationship was more than a friendship?

I was having a big conflict with God, because now I'd fallen for Julie. I had this really horrible, horrible evening when I was talking to God about it. Thanks to my good Sunday school I did trust God enough to argue and say, "How could you make me this way and then forbid it? I am this way. I am gay. If I can't be gay and Christian, then I'm not going to be able to be Christian. That would make me tremendously sad." I didn't know how not to be Christian. I hadn't had any success with that, either. I was just really sad about it. I'm crying and tossing pillows and again I say, "How could you make me this way and then forbid it? Are you mocking me? Are you laughing at me?"

God didn't let me down. As clear as a person talking to me I heard, "That's the dumbest thing I've ever heard. You've had nothing but love in Sunday school and from people around the church. You know I would never hurt you." And it just all fell apart--for the good.

I was to join the church on December 5th of 1982 with the other new members. The day before joining I went to talk to the pastor. He was the second straight person I would tell I was gay. I knew him by then, mostly through his preaching and teaching the Bible Study. I told him about myself in case he would want to stop me from joining. I really liked him and unfortunately, I think I was willing to accept his judgment on this. It's hard to explain why, but I just really felt compelled to tell him I was gay. I went to my appointment with him that day. I told a long story about myself and I included that I was gay and then I just cried. He helped tremendously. The main battle was with God and God won, thankfully. This conversation with the pastor was merely the "clean-up"--a human face put to God. Thank God!

After the crying, I said that I knew I couldn't be gay and Christian (even though I was thinking God had told me it was okay). My pastor replied with, "Why do you think you can't be gay and Christian?" Then it was over. That was the end. That was the human face. I had been crying, and then I just started to smile. I said I really didn't know why. I guessed that this was why I was there, so someone could tell me it was okay. I was lacking confidence, but aware that I was after all, both gay and Christian. He was affirming. He said that everything he had read said that being gay was just another way that humans were created, and there was nothing wrong with being gay. So, when I joined the Methodist Church, I was "out," at least to the pastor. I knew that every time he preached grace, every time he preached inclusion, even when he was talking about our sins and how we needed to take a look at those and confess them, I always knew I was included as a full human being. Homosexuality was not my sin. I regained my confidence as a part of the church family.

Next I told Julie. The day of my appointment with the pastor was also my birthday. The pastor suggested that I tell Julie, because he knew we were friends. At first I protested, but he encouraged me. I went and told her right away.

Did you know that she was gay, as well?

Julie's more in the middle of the continuum so she'd dated guys, more of a bisexual. She had never thought of herself as gay. However, it was my birthday and she had planned a surprise party that night. It was wonderful. By this time she had fallen for me as well. Within a few weeks we were a couple, but it took time for her to sort out feelings and sense of identity.

How long were you together before you decided to take a sabbatical year from teaching?

I took my sabbatical in 1990, so it must have been not quite eight years. I was a high school algebra teacher and basketball coach. Julie was a social worker. We bought a home--a new house with a big back yard. We had a dog named Caurie. As far as our families go, some of them took a little longer to be understanding, but they were never, never mean. We started with "tolerate" and wished we could have moved a little more quickly to "celebrate," but we never suffered from our families. We were really active at the church. Julie was on several committees, she did a lot of program projects. We were still in the Tuesday night Bible study. That was our life. The church was truly our community. We worked in different towns and drove home to Edinboro. One year, while celebrating our anniversary at "our" homecoming parade, we realized that most of the people that we recognized were the Methodists. This was who we knew the best.

You told me that you had changed your focus in 1990. Go into that, and how it changed your life.

I had a sabbatical year from teaching. I had no further goals in teaching than to be a classroom teacher, because that's what I enjoyed and found meaningful. When I had the opportunity to take that year off, Julie asked me, "In your wildest dreams, what would you like to do?" I replied that I thought I might like to go to seminary to study God, the Bible and theology. Julie was actually the one to put in the call to get some catalogues sent to the house. It was during basketball season, and I was busy. I inquired into two different United Methodist seminaries. I came to choose Garrett-Evangelical which is a United Methodists seminary in Evanston, Illinois. Since my plan was a one year sabbatical, and I didn't feel called to ministry, I just wanted to take the best teachers. I was an educator, so I wasn't worried about the subject titles. I knew I wanted to take the Bible survey that all the first year students take. I had a Bible class each quarter. Other classes included history, evangelism, theology and social justice. I had a great, great experience. It was hard for me, because as a math major in college I had not written that many papers, but I accomplished the task and really enjoyed the thinking and questioning that it required.

I was not "out" as lesbian when I was teaching school all those years in a small town, but it was one of those "secrets" that many people knew. Much later, when I asked former students, they would relate that they "knew since we were in the fourth grade." Everyone knew Julie. Faculty and students would ask about her. It was a discretionary practice--to know but never say out loud. At seminary I never said it out loud to anybody until January or February, when I told one friend.

I took one class called Systematic Theology. Normally first-year students don't sign up for this and certainly people who are there for "a lark" don't take it. Several people tried to talk me out of it, but I wanted to see what these theological people knew. That seemed like the heart of it.

Thank God again that I took that class. Dr. Dwight Vogel taught it. It ended up being too hard for me. I struggled along. It took me too long to read the material, because I didn't have the same vocabulary as the others. I wrote the papers to the best of my ability. One time Dr. Vogel asked me if I was okay with my grade, because it wasn't great and he was checking to see if I'd be able to hang in there. I told him I did the best I could, but I knew it was shallow. He smiled when I suggested that I had not fooled him. It was a great class. The teacher would always start the class with a hymn that went with whatever the theological topic was for the day. With my background in church, the hymns connected with my experience.

In the middle of that quarter he assigned a paper and the title was "What Does It Mean To Be Fully Human From a Christian Perspective?" I had been happy being gay here and Christian there. I began to realize that I had kept these two aspects of my identity compartmentalized by not being "out"--open about whole self. I was allowing the comfort level of other people to dictate how I presented myself and my family. I thought I was happy in that, but this paper, "What Does It Mean To Be Fully Human From a Christian Perspective," hit me hard. I really had a meltdown. In preparation for the paper, I had read the materials, made and studied my notes, but I was stuck. I slowly realized from the taught Christian perspective I wasn't human. I tried various ways to begin. As a teacher myself I thought, "Just write that first paragraph or that first page and it will start to flow." It did not work. I was paralyzed with pain at first.

One topic I could include in this paper was the imago Dei or being created in the image of God. That is when God and I just went to a deeper level. I admitted what Christianity had done to me as a gay person. Having compartmentalized my own identity, I wouldn't have suggested I was created gay before. Yet, now I was thinking about being created in the image of God and gay--that this was something of God. I believed that was true, but I really hadn't thought that deeply about it. When I was asked to consider this from a Christian perspective, I felt an anger that I had never felt before. That was one of my false starts--I told myself I just had to write down what I was upset about by Saturday night or Sunday morning, but that didn't work. I fought with this paper all weekend, twenty-four hours a day. I would just say, "How would I know that I'm human from a Christian perspective, when according to others I'm neither human nor Christian?" I wrote something to that effect, and it was painful to admit that I was even responding and allowing people to treat me in a way that was neither human nor Christian.

This was just incredibly painful, and by Sunday evening I was exhausted. I called on my next-door neighbor in the dorm. She knew I'd been struggling all weekend, but she didn't know why. I don't know how bad I looked, but when I suggested going out for something to eat, she just dropped her work, called another friend, and we all went out. I just decided, "I'm not writing that paper. I'm on sabbatical. I don't need to write it." It was a real turning point for me in integrating being gay into my theology, and knowing for certain that one can be both gay and Christian. It was profoundly simple. "Jesus loves the little children, all the children of the world." I became confident that when one investigates it deeply, it is okay to be gay.

When I went to class on Monday, with no paper, I cheered myself by thinking, "So what. I'm on sabbatical. Now I won't have to write the last paper either. I'm home free." As usual, we began class with a hymn. I don't remember what it was, but it just unraveled my pretense--again because I feel so spiritually connected during the hymns. When I told the professor I didn't have the assignment, he said that skipping an assignment meant failing the course. He suggested I at least turn in something brief. I said that I understood, but I could not write this paper. No hard feelings. On Thursday when the class was to meet again, he suggested that perhaps I could do the paper orally in a meeting with him. This was a ray of hope for me. I immediately began to justify my situation, telling him I had read the material, I had prepared my notes, and I had tried to put my thoughts on paper. So when he asked me when we could meet for the oral exam, I told him, "As soon as possible, because I don't want you to think I have just blown this off."

We met the next afternoon. In the first ten minutes, I got it out that I was gay. He had realized it was something. He had seen that there was something blocking me. During the oral exam, we talked about the assignment--several aspects of being human from a Christian perspective. One of these was being created in the image of God. I earned a 'B' or 'B' minus. More importantly, it was a turning point for me.

Later I had to do the final paper for the course. This one wasn't hard at all. I have thanked this professor, and I have teased him by saying he ruined my life. I had been so complacent, now I was sensitive and aware of a need to be more open about my whole self. A few weeks later, sometime in March, I came out to the whole seminary community. I thought it was a teachable moment for my friends who would be pastors. Perhaps one day they would be as helpful with a parishioner who was gay as my home pastor had been. I really thought I would go back and be a teacher forever. However, I went home, taught another year and felt a call to ministry. I would return to seminary.

Again, I'm thankful to God. As I felt compelled to come out to my pastor and later to my professor, I was blessed with affirmation by both of them. It seems that my call to ministry has always included that I would pursue it as an "out" lesbian. Before I ever joined the Church and before I felt a call to ordained ministry I had already told people about myself. I couldn't go backwards. Even though I can tell some sad stories about being out in the United Methodist Church, Julie's a wonderful person and I've been able to live with my partner and not hide.

How did the process of applying for ministry play out for you as an out gay person?

During my three years as a Master of Divinity student, I went to see my District Superintendent to begin the candidacy process for ordination. It wasn't my plan to come out to him at that time. I would have come out before I was ordained, but at the moment I wanted many people to know me, like me and become invested in me before I faced them with the fact that I was gay. I wanted them to enter the dilemma--here is someone with a calling and gifts for ministry, but also happens to be gay--should that automatically eliminate her? Having achieved a seminary education would enhance my abilities and show my commitment.

I was unaware that this District Superintendent already knew I was lesbian when we had our first meeting. We had a pleasant conversation about church and faith journey. I was ready to be assigned a mentor pastor and pursue the steps of discerning my call. However, the DS became noticeably uncomfortable. He shifted in his chair and changed directions. He said, "You have stressed that you have lived in this area all of your life--then perhaps you know that there are rumors about you." I didn't want to be dismissed easily, so I replied, "Really." I made him ask directly whether I was gay. When he did, I used language from the United Methodist Book of Discipline and said, "I am a self-avowed practicing homosexual. That is what I was when I was called and that is what I will be when I am ordained." I was turned down specifically because I told him I was gay. When a new DS came to our district I went again--to make him aware and invested. I was turned down three times, altogether.

How did you deal with that whole experience and where did you go from there?

I was still a student in seminary. Julie and I enjoyed the affirmation of that community. We had a lot of successes at Garrett-Evangelical, breaking the silence at times, breaking down barriers at times. It's not to our credit--several barriers had been softening because of people before us, but because we were so out and so well liked we were able to reap the harvest of those who had gone before us.

Two accomplishments were that I was the first openly gay/lesbian MDIV student to graduate--and that's not to dishonor all those faithful gay people before me who were so committed to their calling and so dedicated that they submerged what they needed in order to honor that calling--but Julie and I were out the whole time. Another barrier was that as a family, Julie and I were not allowed in the seminary housing. A group of students and faculty took up the cause and it was changed. This had been questioned for years, but we were a face to the issue. Rather than "Should homosexual families be allowed?" it became, "Why can't Sue and Julie live in the apartments with the rest of us?" When I graduated, it was a very emotional moment for me--I loved having a Masters of Divinity, having that education and being a part of the Garrett community. As I came across the stage in this big United Methodist church in Evanston to get my diploma from the president and the registrar, a standing ovation began. I just teared up and let myself feel it. What remains as the best part is not the glory of that, but the teachable moment. By the time the clapping was over, even those who were unaffected by me or what I did, even my enemies and their families, were informed what was going on. The ovation was only in appreciation of what I had offered Garrett. I didn't know my future, but it was wonderful.

You had your Masters of Divinity and were feeling good about your contribution to some kind of understanding in this issue. What was next for you?

Julie and I stayed two more years in Evanston, and it is nice to be in Chicago where it's easier to be gay, or at least to be gay and Christian. I really felt a calling to go to places where there is no church available to gay and lesbian people. So, we went back to Pennsylvania to our old home. We tried to go to our home church, but there was a different pastor and that was difficult. We connected with progressive friends and tried to work within the United Methodist Church. Unlike Garrett, now we were the seed planters, not the harvesters. The harvesters are still to come. It was tough.

Julie and I used to say we were kicked out of four churches in three years, and every story is painful and different. That kind of sums it up. Of course, the most painful place is our former church home in Edinboro. It is the hardest one to describe with no one tangible moment to illustrate the situation. When bad things would happen to us in other churches, we were consoled a little by the fact that they did not know us. We felt that we shouldn't have even been there. We should have been at our home church, but weren't welcome there either.

Share the one story of the church where you were so willing to participate

and serve and met with hurt and rejection, instead.

In the fall of 1999 we were without a church again and we were raking leaves on a Sunday morning. We had our week-ends open--kind of pretending we did not care. We were choosing the path of least pain. However, with Christmas coming, I wasn't sure that being without church would still be the path of least pain.

With Advent we started going to a little church in the next town up the road. We went to the early service which was small. We didn't participate as much as we had before, but we could at least have Sunday morning worship. The pastor was a good preacher who prepared her sermons well. The music was fine. The pastor was kind to us introducing us as partners in the early service. We appreciated that. It was good to be somewhere on Sunday morning.

In January, she asked me if I would be a lay reader in the service. They had been asking for volunteers. By early February I was in the front, reading Scripture and offering prayers. It felt right. You feel more like you belong when you participate. The next month, when it would be my turn again, I saw in the bulletin that my name was not there. I thought that was odd, but wondered if there were five people instead of four. Maybe I'd counted wrong. I decided that after church I'd ask where my name was.

But before church got out that day, during the joys and concerns, someone raised his hand and said. "I have a concern. I'd like us to pray for this church. I want to pray for the meeting tomorrow night. I want to pray that everyone remembers that we're a Bible-believing church." I knew in my heart what that was about. This is what homosexuals fear, that we're not welcome. "We're a Bible believing-church" really means "our church is in danger and we need this meeting to judge and kick out the gay people."

There were some very nice people in this service. As I was leaving that day, I saw the man who assigned the worship leaders. I took hold of his hand and would not let go. I asked, "Harry, what's going on?" He gave me some side-show answer, so I asked him, "What's the meeting tomorrow night?"

Then he admitted it was about me not being a reader any more. Part of the trouble, obviously, was started by some of the people in that first service, but the backup was from the people in the big service at eleven--people we'd never met.

Within six weeks there were several different meetings. The pastor had tried to stop this attack, but was not able. She invited the District Superintendent to come and help stop it. Instead, the DS just let it happen. Legally, you could not do this to lay people in the United Methodist Church, but the DS let them pass a rule that homosexual persons could not lead in worship, be on a committee with a vote, or teach Sunday school.

Julie and I didn't have any place else to go to church so we just kept going there. We just thought, "Teach your own Sunday school!" If we're not in church on Sunday, we don't know who we are! We just had to think that the congregation did not know us. Perhaps it would get better. After a while, people started coming to us--quietly--saying, "I am sorry about that rule. It makes me angry." Another said, "My brother was gay. We know that he was a Christian as well."

I tried to get people to tell these stories more widely, because that rule could be changed again. Perhaps as parishioners came to know about others, the rule could be dismissed. Another leader in the church came to me and said that her sister was a lesbian, and that her name was very similar to mine. She added that this seemed like a sign that she needed to get involved in being more helpful--helping the Church to be more open. We attended for another year, and then we couldn't do it any more.

Because so many of us who are gay and lesbian just disappear quietly, I decided to attend an Administrative Board meeting. There were fourteen people there and I told them that Julie and I had to leave. It was the anniversary of their vote to exclude us out of full participation. The hardest part of the meeting was that I perceived that over half of the people in that room, plus the pastor, were sympathetic to me. Nothing I could say would make any of them speak up for me. I couldn't quite tell who the antagonistic people were--they were just going to endure it and be glad I was gone. I was making my plea as to ways we were good for that church. We had brought our neighbor kids. I had been on the welcoming committee. There was no response. I mentioned stories of the Gospel--about Jesus, loving your neighbor, the Good Samaritan. Still there was no response. When I finally said, "This just isn't fair. What you have done is create a second class citizen in God's house. There isn't a second class citizen, no back of the bus, no back door in God's house."

It just seems odd to me, to this day, that was when I got a rise. I was using "American citizen" language. My chief antagonist in there finally was exposed when he said, "We never meant to make you feel that way." I was stunned, thinking--what are you talking about? I was thinking it should have offended you when I said you haven't followed the Gospel, but that was okay with you. Now you have been offended by my claim of being treated as a second class citizen. You do not value the Gospel inclusion, yet you get to stay! You get to stay and be in this church. I believe that God has taught us through Jesus Christ to be inclusive and I do not get to participate if I stay. We left that church.

The biggest regret I have about moving back to Chicago was leaving my

BYKOTA group. "BYKOTA" stood for "Be Ye Kind, One to Another" from Ephesians 4:32. This was a group I started for gay Christians. We had met for four years. We built community and had our own traditions beginning. I hated to leave that group. People like these, people without church, are the ones I feel accountable to--that I cannot just quit.

You are the outreach person for the Reconciling Ministries Network of the United Methodist Church. Tell me what that's about.

I believe that people who desire a church community should be welcome for worship and participation. I believe that in the United Methodist Church I have a place to stand and make my argument for the total inclusion of gay and lesbian people in the life of the church. At its finest, the United Methodist Church is a grace preaching church. The communion table is open--it is God's table--no one can say who is welcome or not welcome. I love that about the Methodist Church. I also love the hymn book. Sometimes when I've been out speaking I run into "Bible bullies," and I have been in worship services where my defenses are up during the preaching. However, I have never met a "hymnal bully." Even when I am in the most hateful, anti-gay place, when we sing the songs, my defenses come down. I feel like God has a light shining on me as I sing the words in the hymn. I feel spiritually connected and able to worship God.

Coming to Reconciling Ministries is a way to help the United Methodist Church remember its finest parts and stop its bigotry against this category of people. We offer hope for full inclusion to the Lesbian, Gay, Bisexual, and Transgender community as they seek a place within the church. We teach within good Methodist tradition the application of the quadrilateral sense of how God is being revealed, even now. Yes, there is scripture--let's look at it as a whole--it is primary. But we can trust tradition, experience, and reason to tell us more. In Reconciling work we encourage people to tell their stories. Their experience matters--the learning they have about homosexuality being an orientation and not just a behavior. Our experience of God within families show the Spirit is present. These stories matter and they tell us about God.

In Reconciling work, we encourage people to trust God with their being. We also work to create church for people. We are conscientious about going places where we haven't been before. We try to ease the isolation of those who are in harsh places. While some people have found Reconciling Congregations to attend, it can be tempting to rest and forget that others still need our ministry. This takes many good people who volunteer in their local areas.

We also work at the national level to affect change within the UMC. At General Conference in 2004 we initiated a campaign we called "Watermarked" in which we proclaimed, "We are permanently and powerfully a part of the family." Our baptism is our watermark, our sign of authenticity. The gay community truly values that word authentic. The Watermark is a sign of authenticity, but it also cannot be erased, no matter who says we're not good enough for God. Whoever says that is a liar. We are permanently and powerfully part of the family.

At the Reconciling Convocation in 2005 we said, "We are Gay, Lesbian, Bisexual, Transgender, friends, family and allies making disciples for Jesus Christ for the transformation of the world." What is significant about that is that we mean it and that it is also the mission of the United Methodist Church. We are United Methodists, so our mission as Reconciling people is the same as the denominations--making disciples for Jesus Christ for the transformation of the world.

You said that the hymns have been comforting for you--are there scriptures that help you in day-to-day living or when the going gets tough?

Especially in this time after the Judicial Council Ruling 1032 that gave permission to pastors to deny membership to homosexuals at the pastors' discretion, Psalms 30 and 31 are helpful. We have had rulings against gay clergy and their supporters for a long time, but with this ruling the lay people took a hit. The man who was barred from membership was a gay man. That pastor has it all categorized in the language of sin. The pastor reveals no understanding of sexual orientation as a way of being fully human, being created in the image of God, having the capacity to love others. The Church says you can be homosexual, but can't have the same capacity to love others that makes you human. In this lament season, Psalm 30 has that verse about how "we may weep for the night, but joy comes in the morning."

My favorite Psalm when times are tough is Psalm 31, and it's written for gay people. "In the Lord, do I seek refuge, let me never be afraid." Other favorites are from the Gospel--the Good Samaritan, the parable of the 100 sheep. When 99 return, the good Shepherd goes to find the lost. When I was young I was taught to trust that I could not get lost from God--God would come and find me. I like the way Jesus is present with the people, how he teaches and uses parables. I like John 10:10-28 especially when Jesus says, "My sheep hear my voice... No one will snatch them out of my hand." Later, in John 14, Jesus says that after he is gone, "God will give you another Advocate, to be with you forever." "Advocate" is a meaningful word in the gay community. Jesus was speaking of the Holy Spirit--a comforter and the Spirit of Truth. We hope to live in truth.

You wanted to make a couple of comments about the Church splitting.

In this work, I am privileged to go where I have been invited. These are usually friendly audiences. One of the questions I get asked a lot is, "How do you stay in it?" One of the questions I receive is "How do you keep going?" People are tired of defending themselves. We really resist the idea that church is a place where we fight. Some folks have suggested that maybe we should just split the church. Sometimes the suggestion is offered very sincerely. The conservative group, Good News, promotes an "amicable split." However, when one is being forced out, it does not feel "amicable."

On the other hand, there are times when I think the phrase "amicable separation" sounds so restful. I wouldn't have to suffer the attacks of others. I wouldn't have to argue my position. If the denomination splits, then I could go to one side and rest. I could stop explaining who I am and why I want to come to church.

However, the group on the other side is mistaken if they think they will be able to rest from discussion on this issue. This very Sunday there are going to be new babies in those churches, and they are going to baptize those babies. Those babies are going to grow up and the adults will be so proud of their children in Sunday school and choir. The children will become teenagers and be in confirmation class. One day, when they get to be twenty or so, some of them will realize that they are gay or lesbian. Then, these children are not going to want to leave the church that taught them about Jesus. They, and maybe their family members, will take up the cause for inclusion within that congregation. So I will not really be resting. I already know that in twenty years all those split-off congregations will be in the same place they are today--people within their own churches wanting to remain as "permanently and powerfully part of the family," promised in their baptism as babies. My obligation is helping congregations be honest about our families now. Perhaps we can avoid separation or splitting as part of the UM experience today. I offer 1 Corinthians 12: 12- 26, that we are all the body of Christ and we need everyone.

Once in an interview for a church position, I was asked what my "agenda" would be if I came to that church. I didn't know if they knew I was gay, but the word "agenda" can be loaded--the gay agenda, you know. I told them that my agenda was to help people know Jesus. It has been a tremendous, positive life force for me, and I want people to have the experience in church that I had.

This would be a good time for the "ring" story. At Convocation you came to the Parents' meeting and told the story of your mentors in the church where you grew up. They were Mr. and Mrs. Flanagan. It was a very moving and love-filled story that bears sharing as a part of this interview.

As I said earlier, growing up at church, even if I was hit-and-miss in Sunday school, I saw the Flanagans every week from grade one through eleven. They didn't have their own children, and after a while we realized that we were their kids. They poured themselves into our well-being. They were examples of loving Christians. When I was in the eleventh grade, it was announced that they were leaving. I was devastated. Before then, I had thought it was strange that bad news could cause a person to cry almost immediately. Now I was having that experience. They had been such a big part of my belonging to that church. I was chosen out of the bell choir to give them our gift. I felt honored by this, but when the time came I was crying so much that I could hardly speak. It was hard to see them go. I kept wishing there was something I could give them. There were so many people giving them really nice things.

I had gotten my high school class ring just before Christmas in 1971. In those days if you got yellow gold, the ring cost twenty-seven dollars, and if you got white gold it was thirty-one dollars. It was a hard, hard decision to pay that extra four dollars--it was a lot of money. I had paid that extra four dollars, and I had that ring in my possession for three days.

I knew the Flanagans were loading their moving truck on Saturday morning. I had to go to basketball practice that morning, and it was the opposite direction from their house, so I got up really early that morning. I walked to where they were loading their truck. I had that ring three days and it was precious to me, and I gave it to Mrs. Flanagan and Mr. Flanagan. They knew not to give it back. I'm sure they didn't want to take it from me, but they knew not to refuse it. They were gracious and touched by this. All through the years, they offered stability and knowledge that God loves me. The ring was a small token in return.

I was in touch with them, once in a while over the years. I enjoyed remembering that my ring was with them. Two years ago, I went to visit them in Dayton, Ohio. I was nearby for reconciling work and was a little afraid to call, not knowing if they were still healthy or alive. I called and they were both at home. I went for lunch.

They were such loving friends in listening to my story. They mentioned a favorite relative of theirs who was gay. I told them about my reconciling work and shared with them examples of my ministry. They had known before that I was gay, but even so I was a little afraid. Even when you are sure a significant friend will be supportive, it still feels risky to be so vulnerable.

I learned a story of theirs that I had not known previously. Before they came to my church they had tried to adopt a child. They were lined up with social services to adopt a child. However, in the late 1950s if they wanted to do this, Mrs. Flanagan had to stay home and be a full time mother. Together they told the adoption agency that she could not stay home because she had children at the church. I was newly touched by their sacrifice. I never knew that part of the story, but I had felt it all my life. Perhaps this helps to explain my sense of calling--to go to places where people do not know that God loves them.

They retired several years ago. They were at that point in life when they were giving things away--meaningful gifts from their life in ministry. When I was about to leave their house, Mrs. Flanagan said they had something of mine that they wanted to give back. They had thought of it before, but had never wanted to hurt my feelings. Now it seemed like the right time. I knew exactly what she had. I told her if she knew where the ring was I would love to have it, because now it was more theirs than mine and I would think of them whenever I wore it. She knew right where it was.

The two human beings who were God's disciples helped me to know that I am loved and that I belong no matter what--I am human, from a Christian perspective.

I had this brand new ring on my finger every day at the 2004 General Conference. It was my armor and it protected me. It was my comfort and it gave me hope.

I have been so incredibly blessed with people coming into my life at the right time. God has really blessed me and I am truly thankful.

Ruth and Naomi

Honoring Vows

This is one of those interviews in which the women involved did not want their real names used. The reasons will become obvious as the story unfolds. When I asked them if they had names they would like to use instead, they said they had talked about it and had decided on Ruth and Naomi. At first, I thought they might be teasing, but they explained that the Biblical story of Ruth and Naomi was special for them. It lifted up the Old Testament women's beautiful and loyal friendship and the story had been read at these modern day women's commitment ceremony. The names Ruth and Naomi will be used throughout their interview.

I first came in contact with Ruth when she was enrolled at a university where I worked in the bookstore. She would come into the bookstore and visit when she had supplies to pick up. She was in a preparatory program for a vocation in Christian ministry. As the time approached for her graduation from the university and her leaving for seminary, I felt her seeking a little closer relationship with me. It was general knowledge that I had a gay son and was open about discussing that fact. At first, she just shared information about her brother who was gay and suffering from AIDS, but I felt like she might want to share more. Eventually, she showed up at an annual Valentine party that our parent support group hosted for the gay community every February, and I knew her situation without her telling me more.

We kept in contact over the years through Christmas cards. Hers always showed photos of her and her beloved puppies. She would call me from time to time when she was going to be in town and we'd have lunch. She shared her struggles in being a lesbian minister and trying to make sense of her role in the local church.

I ran into her at a Reconciling Congregation's workshop that we were both attending in a nearby city. In our conversation, she shared the news of her relationship with Naomi.

This is mostly about her struggles, but also about a special relationship.

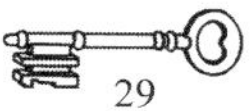

A person's childhood faith roots are usually significant in shaping the direction of one's adult journey. Could you share that part of your life?

Ruth: My first experience with church, and how I saw God, was going with my grandma. She shaped my image of God. When I saw the caring and kindness in her life, I knew that this was the caring and kindness that I was supposed to show. I knew that this was the way to be a Christian--by being kind and caring. I started going when I was little. I was probably eight or nine. She took me to the Mother/Daughter banquets as well as to Sunday school. There was a short time when I didn't go, but I later became active in my teens through youth group. My grandmother had laid a foundation for me, and I knew it was important in her life, so I wanted to keep going. There was a significant thing that happened to me in youth group. The pastor asked me to do the devotion one evening. When I did it, I had kind of a special feeling. I just felt connected to God in a special way.

What happened after that?

I went from high school to junior college where I took all the Associate of Arts courses. I graduated from the community college and then started working part time in a taco shop. After working there for two years, I knew the business world wasn't the world I wanted to be in, the whole taco shop experience, you know. I was still trying to figure out what to do. I was still active in the church but was keeping God at a distance, not wanting to admit what God might be calling me to do.

So would you say that there was a specific moment when you knew you were being called into the ministry by God?

Probably the experience when the pastor asked me to give the devotions for our youth group. After I gave the devotions, the pastor asked me how I'd liked doing it, and I said that it felt like a natural thing, but there still wasn't a total acceptance of my call. It took my working in the taco shop for two years and not being satisfied with what was going on. I was frustrated and felt like I wasn't getting anywhere. I finally decided that God's call had been there starting back in high school. It was kind of a gradual thing after that. Kind of a gradual acceptance: "Yeah, this is what I'm supposed to be doing."

When I first met you, you were going to a four-year college. Did you start out in a course toward the ministry at that time?

At the four-year college where I met you they have a program for ministerial students. I think they called it "religious studies," or something like that. When I got into my courses, it seemed like the right thing to be doing, diving into Scriptures and studying the history of Scripture.

Did you already know that you were a lesbian at this point in time?

You know, it's kind of funny. I kept a journal and in 1984--I can look back and see that--you probably hear this all of the time from people--I kind of knew. I just didn't want to admit it. I knew, but I didn't want to know, so I just kept ignoring it. Even in high school I remember when some of the girls got hold of a Playgirl magazine. They were getting all excited about the male figures. Even then I thought, "What's the big deal about this?" There was nothing there. Once you finally do the internal struggling, you realize why you didn't get it. But, there were those inklings shortly after I was in high school.

Did that struggle ever spill over into reconciling your call to the ministry with being a lesbian?

In seminary I was still kind of struggling with it, but I finally just said, "Okay." I talked to a friend about how to deal with the issue of integrity in being a local pastor. How do you continue to authentically be who you are? At the time I don't believe I resolved the integrity issue. I just went ahead and took the vows of ordination and celibacy like other single ministers. I had talked to some people about it and decided to go from there. I felt after my ordination that I could serve and be who I am. I just didn't need to tell the church who I am. It was really a struggle. I didn't know who could be trusted, either in the local church or in the Annual Conference. I think just being single in the local church is a struggle enough. With the issue of sexual misconduct being focused on so strongly by the United Methodist Church, it is hard for single women to make relationships with men outside of the church. Then add to that the complexity of being a lesbian. It makes it even harder. Not being in a relationship with a man caused problems in my first church. One of the women who liked the previous pastor a lot decided to start spreading the rumor that I was a lesbian. I actually had to go to the District Superintendent and tell him that this rumor was being spread. Luckily, he never asked me if I was or if I wasn't. He just took it as a personal attack against me that was being spread by an unhappy parishioner. This was the first and only time when I served local churches that I was faced with the issue. It was really a frightening experience because from that time forward, it was always at the forefront of my mind that someone could accuse me of being a lesbian. So I had to be really careful about the people I hung around with.

What was it like in the local church after you were through seminary?

It was really hard. My mom knew I was struggling with the problems I was having with being in the local church. She always stood behind me and supported me just like my grandma did. I think she knew that in some way there were difficulties associated with being single. For me that revolved around the fact that I took this vow of celibacy, and then went out into the local church in a small town in the rural Midwest. There's scary stuff to be wary of. Like, if you are associated with gay people, you always have to be looking over your shoulder. Celibacy in the single life and fidelity in marriage were required to stay in the pastorate. Like I said, I always had to be wary of being associated with gay people. I always felt like I had to be looking over my shoulder. One of my friends, who I learned I could trust, told me that as long as people don't know what you are doing in your private life, you can be who you are. This helped me with my ordination vows.

Other than the matter of having to be so careful, did you enjoy pastoring a local congregation?

I really enjoyed it. I really enjoyed preaching and being involved with the people, but I had to separate my two lives. My private life was my private life, and my public life was my public life. I kind of focused on my public life. It made it much easier for me to exist in the local congregation. Looking back, I realize how unhealthy it was, but it's the way that local congregations look at their pastor. They really don't want to know about their pastor's social life. I really didn't have a social life, being in a small town. All my life seemed to revolve around the church. I went to ball games, concerts, and plays, to be there for people who were in them.

I found that the longer I was in the pastorate, the bolder I got. Homosexuality was a hot-button topic in the worldwide church, so I felt like I could begin to address the issue a little bit. I guess it was my way of beginning to change the local church, one person at a time. In one of my last pastorates, I made friends with two gay men. The whole community knew that they were gay. I was their pastor and their friend. They let me talk about myself and be who I was with them. I was able to gain some freedom through this. It was also the first time I felt comfortable leading a Bible study on homosexuality. I knew I was biased in my views but I tried to treat both sides fairly so that no matter what side of the issue people were on, they could feel they were being heard.

It was during that time that one of the people in the church told me her brother was gay and that he was active in a big church far away from his home community. He had never told their parents. I could see the relief on her face that she could actually tell someone else and could find some support within the church.

This was also a difficult time in the church, because the two gay men that I had become friends with were the victims of blatant discrimination. The youth group I worked with in the town wanted to raise some money for a trip, so they had an auction. People could hire them to do work. The two men wanted to hire some boys to come and work at their house to clean the yard and trim trees--stuff like that. Someone told me they had overheard the parents of the boys say, "If they think we are going to let them hire our boys..." So the parents outbid the men on all the boys except for one, whose parents didn't care. I was proud of the youth leader, though. She made a work date with the two men, and the whole youth group had to go help instead of just one or two of the boys. This incident reminded me, as if I needed to be reminded, that I needed to be careful about whom I was with and what I said and what I did. The incident didn't keep me from enjoying the congregation, however.

There are two things that I continue to miss about the local church. One is being involved in the spiritual lives of young people and the other is the sacraments. I loved and still long to serve communion and baptize people.

Why did you decide to take a leave from the United Methodist Church and from your pastorate if you enjoyed being in that role?

I still have my credentials, but I decided that the struggle was just too much. I just kind of got weary. I got weary of being in the church--being one thing at one time and another at another time takes its toll. I wasn't being fair to myself. I wasn't being fair to the people in my congregation, and I wasn't being fair to God. I was putting so much energy into the struggle that I wasn't taking care of myself. I just needed time to regroup.

The struggle with my call to ministry caused me to question what I was supposed to be doing. I felt like my struggles in the local church indicated that maybe I had misinterpreted God's call. I believe that this time off has helped me to see once again that the call to ministry is still there. I just need to figure out how to live it out and be in relationship with Naomi.

Were you angry at the Church and the rules set down in the Book of Discipline--the rules forbidding ordination of openly gay Christians?

Oh, I was angry at, I guess, lots of different things. I was angry at society for the stigmas it puts on gays and lesbians, I was angry at the Church that it had such a stance. I was angry at the people in the local churches that I served, as they were the ones who put forth the legislation at Annual Conference or General Conference about gays and lesbians being excluded from the Church. Never in that whole process of laying that foundation with my Grandma have I ever felt rejected by God, or that being a lesbian would cause me to be rejected there. If I could go back and tell my grandma, who is now deceased, that I am a lesbian, she'd take it in stride. It was that love and acceptance from my grandma as a child, and as I was growing up, that caused me never to consider that I wasn't loved and accepted by God.

I had asked you to think about some scriptures that were meaningful to you in your life. What did you come up with?

I've been thinking about that. I like the story of Esther. She was a strong, bold woman who spoke out against the establishment and the powers that be, to help her people. I think I like this story so much because Esther fought against the stereotypes of her time. Women were to be seen and not heard, but she stepped up and spoke out against the wrongs. I think it's a way for us to look at our lives. We are to step up and stand against the wrongs of the world. I see the gay and lesbian pastors who are taking on the United Methodist Church and saying, "Hey, this is who I am--deal with it," as the Esthers of our time. They are fighting against the stereotypes of today that say gays and lesbians don't make good pastors. I get upset because I see myself as weak but, I know that at this moment in time, I'm doing the best I can.

The other one is from the part of the Bible most Protestant churches don't use. It says in Judith, Chapter 9 verse 11. "For your strength does not depend on numbers nor your might on the powerful, but you are the God of the lowly, helper of the oppressed, upholder of the weak, protector of the forsaken, savior of those without hope."

Through the story of Judith, I am reminded that God is ultimately on my side as a lesbian. I might be oppressed and forsaken by society, but God is on my side, and with God on my side I will not be defeated. That's one of the scriptures I kind of lean on.

Those two are my favorites and "Be still and know that I am God," knowing God's always there if we're just still enough to listen.

Once I left the Church, I had to figure out some means of economic support. I thought maybe being a paraprofessional in the school system would do the job. When I first interviewed for the position, the person who interviewed me wanted me to work with the educable mentally handicapped. When I thought about it I said, "God, there's no way I can do that," but I went down to the classroom and watched the kids, spent some time, and decided I might be able to do this. I just kind of blindly went into it thinking, "Okay, God's going to provide a way." I worked in that area for three years and considered it very much a ministry. Now, I'm out of that classroom and am in a class of behaviorally disabled children. When I first went into the classroom I thought, "O God, there's no way I can work with these kids." Now, I know they are wonderful kids, and I love them. Again, I see it as a ministry. They just need to know that someone loves them and values them just as they are. Even when I was working with youth in the local church, my focus when I was with the kids was to show them that someone, an adult, somewhere in their lives, loved them, cared for them, and worried about them. That has been a part of who I was, especially in a ministry setting--someone who loved them and cared for them just the way they were.

If things changed in the Church, would you go back?

Let me put it this way--it's been in the last three years that I've been asking myself, "Should I go back? What would that mean in the relationship with my partner? How can I fulfill that longing for the local church, now that I'm in a relationship?" I can't throw her away. So, I guess ultimately, if things did change and I could keep my relationship with my partner, then I would be back "in" the local church in a minute.

I want to talk about your relationship with Naomi and maybe hear a

few of her comments on what we've been talking about, but before we do, I want to give you an opportunity to make a few comments about your brother, who died of AIDS in 1994. What do you want to say about that?

I want to say a few things about my brother. At one time I actually asked him how he had contracted the disease. After asking him, I realized it didn't matter. He was my brother, and I was going to love him and help him in any way I could, no matter what. He moved in with me in 1993, because I lived in a large city and he could have access to the medical care he needed. After he moved in with me, we went out to eat with the Pastor Parish Committee Chairperson of one of the churches I was serving at the time. While we were eating, my brother asked if I wanted to try what was on his plate, and I reached over and took a bite off his plate. I knew there was no problem with this, but I guess the Pastor Parish chair had a big problem with it. The next thing I knew I was in the midst of a meeting with the pastor parish chair and the District Superintendent. We made plans to have a joint meeting of the two churches and have Bishop Fritz and Etta Mae Mutti come down and talk about their sons and how they dealt with their sons' diagnoses of AIDS. I felt like the Pastor Parish chair was being an alarmist, and that it was no one's business that my brother had AIDS. The people in the two churches seemed to handle the information okay. All the other churches that I served seemed to be fine with my sharing the information with them about my brother having AIDS.

People seem to have an easier time with AIDS than with homosexuality. True, it started out as a gay men's disease, but there are so many other parts of society involved now that people can see it as a disease, and there is more compassion. Homosexuality brings in people's understanding of what is moral and what is immoral. I believe that people's trouble with handling homosexuality comes directly from our society, that the only good and right sexual relations are within the boundaries of marriage. We can't get past that view. Since gays and lesbians can't get married, their sexual relationships are seen as sinful.

A few minutes ago, you mentioned that you are now in a committed relationship that would complicate your going back into a local church ministry. Let's set that part aside and talk about the relationship itself. How did you meet your partner?

The way I met my partner is that her mother works at the same school where

I work. She came into the classroom one day to pick something up--an eraser or a big pencil--the adaptive stuff for the kids she was working with. There was a short conversation about dogs. Naomi was with her mom, and we waved across the room. Her mom and I had talked about going to a college volleyball game. I thought that would be fun, since we would be cheering for opposite college teams. It didn't work out, as it fell on a weekend when I would be moving, so we decided to try for a basketball game with the same two rivals. We all went, and that was kind of the fateful meeting. We went to a lot more ball games, and that was it.

Naomi, let's focus on your background for a minute. Did you have a similar church upbringing as Ruth's?

Naomi: I grew up in the Christian Church--Disciples of Christ--went to college and stayed away for a while. Later I attended the Unity Church in a metropolitan city. Then I met Ruth, and I started going to her church which is a Reconciling United Methodist Church. Lately, I haven't been going much, because of the "Open Hearts, Open Minds, Open Doors." I don't think it's true. It's just a saying, and I don't believe they live it.

It doesn't make a difference that the church is a Reconciling Congregation?

R: I think, at least for me and most reconciling people, the dilemma is that "Open Hearts, Open Minds, Open Doors" is a campaign--well, let me elaborate. When that first came out, I felt like someone up on high in the United Methodist Church thought that would be a good vision for the United Methodist Church to grow into, so why not throw that out as a campaign slogan and get it out there. Maybe somewhere along the line churches that aren't having their minds and hearts and doors open, will start living that vision. The problem is that it just doesn't resonate with the experience that I have had in my life as a lesbian person. The door isn't open for me. People's hearts aren't open and their minds definitely aren't open in understanding who I am or who anyone else who is different is. You get those exceptions inside the Church and you get those exceptional churches that are trying to overcome all the baggage that the higher church inflicts on them. I admire the Rev. Beth Stroud who came out as a lesbian pastor with a partner, knowing she would probably have to surrender her credentials. People like her will raise awareness in the United Methodist Church and call it to accountability for the ad campaign.

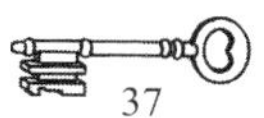

On a lighter note, we have established that you share a love of women's sports, but I know you do scrap-booking as a way of saving memories of your relationship. Do you want to comment on that?

R: That's been kind of fun. I don't do it as much as I'd like. It's been fun to document where we've traveled and what we've done. It's amazing what all we've done in the three-year time period we've been together. I like to look at the albums and remember all the things we have done.

Part of what you have documented in your scrapbook is the holy union that you did. Tell me about that experience.

R: Well, it was within the first six months of our knowing each other that Naomi proposed. I told her I wasn't going to do anything right away, because even though she is hated in the gay community, Dr. Laura says you shouldn't get married until at least a year after the proposal. You can't know somebody in a short time. I told Naomi I wasn't going to do anything until at least a year after the proposal date.

N: I said, "Okay, how about Valentine's Day, 2004, because it's even."

R: Naomi's into numbers. She has a mathematical mind. So, it was Valentine's Day, 2004, which luckily landed on a Saturday. Commitment ceremonies, holy unions, marriages--that's one of those hot topics in the gay communities. For me, I felt like those people I was around, the people I know, and my family, needed to know that I honor and cherish Naomi, and the way I wanted that stated was through a public ceremony. I knew I couldn't do it through the United Methodist Church. Many of the people in the church where I go know that I'm a lesbian. They've been very supportive. We knew the pastor there couldn't be involved because she could be brought up on charges and it would just cause a big ruckus, so we had to look outside the Church. I knew as a Christian that it had to be some kind of religious ceremony. Maybe I buy into that whole heterosexual marriage thing. We found a church, a historic church that didn't have any kind of rules in place. They opened it up and said it was fine to have the ceremony there--we just paid our money like anyone else. We got a mutual friend who was a United Methodist pastor who had left the ministry because she couldn't reconcile the integrity issue. She did the ceremony.

Do you think your relationship is different because of doing the ceremony?

R: Yeah, I feel that before we were just dating, even though we were living together, it was still like just dating. If I'd really wanted to get out of the relationship it would have been easy. I could just say, "Naomi, this isn't working out." After that public ceremony, when I pledged in front of all these people we know that "through better or worse," and all the other vows, I publicly proclaimed that it was now intentional on my part to make it work.

N: I wanted people to know how important Ruth was and that our relationship is real. It made it more real--as real as anybody else's relationship.

Any other comments you want to make?

R: In April of 2003, over that Easter weekend, I went home, and I felt like it was important for my family to finally know. I had told my sister that I was a lesbian. She knew my brother was gay, so I knew she would have no problem supporting me in whatever I was going to do. Naomi had come into my life, and I felt like it was time for my family to finally know who I was. Over that Easter weekend, we had bought my engagement ring. I went home. I told my next oldest brother and his wife. They were great and said they would support me just as long as I was happy. I told my mom, and she wanted to know if I wanted her to tell my dad. That was fine with me because, for whatever reason, I was kind of frightened by that. My mom seemed to take it in. Moms seem to have that intuition. You can probably testify to that. My mom probably knew all along but didn't want to admit it to herself. I bought your first book, *Cleaning Closets*, and I gave it to her. The next time I went home, I noticed it was on the night stand. Shortly after that, the Thanksgiving or Christmas after I told my parents, I asked my mom if it would be okay to bring Naomi home, and she said probably not this time but next time. The next time it was different--my mom made the invitation, and Naomi went home with me.

My mom finally asked me if this was the reason why I had gotten out of the ministry, and she could finally understand the struggle. Now, I just need to figure out what's next.

* *

Ruth is still struggling with her call to ministry and is considering changing denominations to one that will ordain openly lesbian ministers who are in loving relationship with partners.

Bishop Fritz Mutti & Etta Mae

Grace of Steel

The first time I met Fritz and Etta Mae was at an AIDS conference sponsored by one of our hospitals, a local church-related university and some of the local United Methodist Churches. Although I was somewhat in denial about AIDS, on some level I felt that I needed to gather information in any way that I could. I hoped that the disease would not touch our lives in a personal way, but that was a possibility,

I couldn't imagine a bishop and his wife sharing the intimate experience of having had two sons die of AIDS, but they were on the program to do just that. As they stood in front of that gathering of curious persons, my heart went out to them. They told their story with love and grace, placing themselves in a position of vulnerability in the hopes of putting a common face on the disease.

I became better acquainted with Fritz and Etta Mae over the years, and found them to be warm and gracious people. However, underneath that warmth was a strength and determination to use the tragedy of their sons' deaths as a tool to teach others and help them understand and be more loving to those affected by this disease. They braved the political risk involved in Fritz's position in the church to do the right thing.

Tell me about your growing up in the Church.

Etta Mae: I grew up in the Disciples of Christ Church. I was there until Fritz and I were engaged, and then I switched to the United Methodist Church. One question that has been brought up is whether homosexuality was ever mentioned in the church where I grew up. It was not, back in those days. It was never mentioned, and I would say that I grew up in a pretty closed church.

Fritz: I grew up in the Methodist Church in the little town of Hopkins, Missouri. Etta went to a country school, and I went to the town school. We met in high school. Even though we were in two different churches, the youth

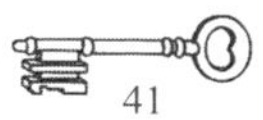

groups met together. We'd go to our ecumenical youth group and then to the movies. That's how we dated.

Fritz, what was your United Methodist Church like?

F: Same as Etta Mae's, not much mention of sexuality at all in those days. All the sexuality education came along later in the United Methodist Church. We had more of that after the seventies, but not in the fifties.

E: What I remember is that people who now would be called gay, and probably were gay, were called sissies. That was my first introduction to persons who were of a different sexual orientation, although we didn't call it that at the time.

That may be true to some extent today, except that kids say, "Oh, that's so gay." That's probably an expression that is used for lots of kinds of behavior that are a little different. Fritz, let's move on to your call to the ministry. How did that happen?

F: I was in engineering school, as a student at Iowa State, when I decided the Lord was calling me into the ordained ministry. I switched from there and went to Central Methodist College where I got a pre-theology degree and then went to seminary. I really think the roots of that calling were back in the local church. My uncle was the Sunday school superintendent for a long time, and my parents always went to church and were very involved. Youth group was always important to us. We sometimes discussed vocation there--what we would do with our lives. When we were in high school, we had a really good pastor who modeled that well for us.

Did you have any one particular event that stands out as a calling for you?

F: I think it was just a gradual unfolding of events. Part of that, as I look back, was my dad's illness. When I was seventeen or eighteen, my dad began to lose control of his hands, and we found out that he had A.L.S. He was sick for about five years before he died, and I guess that got me to thinking about ultimate things. I decided it would be better to work with people than to build airplanes. Etta, do you remember anything specific when I first told you?

E: I remember when he was at Iowa State which was a huge school. He was in classes with hundreds of students and was living in a basement apartment that was dark. He and I were still dating but mostly apart from each other, and he said that things were kind of piling up on him. He said, "I'm a 'nobody' in this school, I'm in this dark apartment, and I'm away from Etta Mae. I don't think this is where I should be in life." I think that was part of it. There were a lot of negative things going on in his life.

F: I was used to getting 'A's in high school, and there I was getting pink slips.

So it was humility that brought you to your knees. All kidding aside, it seems to have been a good fit for you. Let's go on to family life after you two were married. Tell me about your children.

E: We got married in 1959. Our first child was born nine months and two days from when we got married. We hadn't planned it that way. It was Fritz's senior year in college, and I had meant to work. At that time we knew he was going on to seminary. Then we had a baby instead of me having a job. I did work, but I worked at home. I babysat and did typing. This was in seminary. Then we had Fred two and a half years later, while we were still in seminary. So we had Tim and then Fred and then Marty. Marty came two and a half years after Fred, after we got out of seminary.

Is there anything you want to say about any of the congregations you served that might have influenced who you were as a minister?

F: I served a student appointment while I was at Central Methodist College. They were kind of used to having students as their pastors. They were good people, caring people. We still have some good friends from those congregations. They were very supportive and encouraging. I had a student appointment for a couple of years while I was in seminary. Then we came back to Missouri, where we had a three-point circuit up in Northwest Missouri--three small churches, although they were all bigger then than they are now. We were there two years and then went to Savannah, Missouri which was a county seat church north of St. Joseph. That was a really good appointment. We were there for nine years. That really was a formative place for us, and we have some special friends from that place. Our kids started to school at Savannah. During those school years we were involved in a lot of things, active in the community in a lot of different ways.

E: I remember in our first congregation out of seminary, we found the congregation's theology was a little bit different than ours. I think we grew a lot from that experience. We also began to realize that we were going to "hit heads" with people in some congregations.

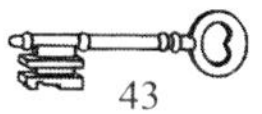

How was their theology different from yours?

E: Well, theirs was just a lot more conservative than ours.

F: Some were biblical fundamentalists, whom I just didn't encounter at all in the church in which I grew up, so I had to learn how to deal with that.

At which seminary were you trained?

F: I went to Garrett-Evangelical in Evanston, Illinois. It was much more open--teaching the critical method of biblical understanding and interpretation. That's really what I grew up with, United Methodist curriculum. The people in the congregation we were in after seminary weren't there in their thinking. They didn't use United Methodist curriculum. What they used was independent curriculum that was more conservative, so we disagreed over that. We weren't talking much about social issues then. We were just on the front edge of the civil rights movement at that time.

E: I do remember one woman coming to interview Fritz for a newspaper article. She asked him what person he admired more than anybody else, and he said Martin Luther King, Jr. She told him that she was thrilled to hear him say that. She hadn't encountered anybody else with that kind of thinking, because of the conservative area we lived in. Part of it was because of King's stance on the issues, and part of it was because he was black.

That's one of those things you don't know has been significant in your life until you look back on it. How many years were you in the ministry before you were asked to run for bishop?

F: After my pastoral appointments, I spent some time in the Conference Office as a conference staff member where I worked with the youth camping program, Christian education, teacher training, and things like that. That appointment lasted six years. I was the Council Director for the Annual Conference for two years. Then we went to Blue Springs for five years to a large suburban congregation with a wonderful ministry. The Bishop asked me to serve as a District Superintendent, and after serving in two different districts, the last in Kansas City. In 1992 I was elected bishop. So, to answer your question, I was in the ministry for thirty years and then was elected bishop. I was bishop in Kansas for twelve years.

All this time you were going about your life and fulfilling your calling as a minister, while Etta Mae, was a pastor's wife, a mother, and an individual pilgrim on her own journey. When did you find out that you had two sons who were gay?

E: I'm not exactly sure when that happened. It was when we were in Blue Springs that we found out, so, probably about 1985. This is when they came out to us, anyway. Fred was working in New York, and Tim was teaching school. We found out through Marty, our youngest, who had been hearing the rumor from some of his high school friends that Fred was gay. So we just asked Fred, and he said that he was gay. He hadn't wanted to tell us, because he wasn't sure how we'd respond. It was then that he said to us, "I think Tim is also." We didn't ask Tim, since he wasn't there at the time, but Tim wrote us later and told us that he was gay. We suspect Fred talked to him and told him what was going on, so he told us.

F: Probably like a lot of parents, we suspected they might be gay from the time they were little boys. The other kids ridiculed Tim, made fun of him, chased him, beat up on him, and Fred had some of that in Junior High. There were the stereotypical things that showed up--they preferred playing with girls, they played "dress-up" as pre- schoolers, they couldn't do sports. So there was just a lot of stereotypical stuff going on. We were still in Savannah when we went to see a counselor in St. Joseph with this hunch. The counselor said they'd grow out of it. When I shared our concerns with my mother, she said the same thing about their outgrowing it.

What happened after you got your sons' confirmations that they were gay? Did you have a lot of processing to do, or had you already done that, since you had suspected that they might be gay?

E: I don't think we told people right away. We told our mothers and a couple of close friends, because we were processing it ourselves. It wasn't a good climate in society for people to know that. It's not the best climate now.

Did your position as a pastor put you in a difficult spot having this happen in your family?

F: Yes, because by then I was involved in the political process as a nominee for bishop, so I didn't know whether that would translate into rejection in the election process or what the consequences would be. In talking to one person who was a delegate to the Jurisdictional Conference he said, "Well, you just have to tell your sons that they're wrong, and they'll just have to change. You just can't stand with it." I told him I wasn't going to do that even if it cost me the election. I didn't get elected that round but did in '92, and by that time they had died.

Let's backtrack a little and fill in the rest of the details of your story. You not only had to adjust to the fact that you had two sons who were gay, but shortly after that revelation you got some disturbing news that there was another crisis to deal with. What was that news?

F: At least we didn't get both pieces of information at the same time. We didn't get a double whammy like a lot of parents do. Since we had suspected that they might be gay from childhood, it wasn't too major a jolt to find out that's what we were dealing with.

How did they let you know that they were sick?

E: Fred called us to tell us that he had pneumonia and called back later to say that it was PCP. We had to ask what that was, and he said it was AIDS pneumonia. Four months later Tim wrote to us to tell us he was HIV positive. It was then that we were coming to the realization that both boys were probably going to die. Most parents don't have to face losing two sons in such a short time. They did die nine months apart.

Were you dealing with HIV or full blown AIDS?

E: With Tim it was AIDS and with Fred it was HIV. At that time they called Tim's illness ARC or AIDS Related Complex, which is an obsolete term now.

F: Before all this, we went to a counselor and talked to her about the fact that Tim and Fred were gay, and we wanted help to process that. Well, the first thing she said to us was, "Aren't you afraid they'll get AIDS?" She didn't process the other with us at all. We hadn't even thought about that at first. We don't know when they got infected.

E: We just assumed that they were infected through sexual contact. We didn't ask them.

You said that they died nine months apart, but how long were they sick?

E: Fred lived three years, but they died nine months apart. Fred was diagnosed in December of 1988 and died in September of '91. Tim was diagnosed in the spring of '89 and died in December of '90. Tim only lived a little over a year and a half, and Fred lived almost three years.

F: Tim didn't even have any symptoms the first year, and then everything hit at once. There were a lot of hospitalizations. All they had then for medication was AZT.

The first time I heard you two tell your family story was at an AIDS Conference I attended in Salina, Kansas. Was that the first time you shared your story, or had you been doing it for a while before that?

E: The first time we told our story was at Blue Springs. Fred had died in September, so they had both died by that time, and this was in January. I remember how hard it was to do the very first time. We were back among people we knew, and it was really hard. The first few times were difficult, but we told it in lots of churches after we moved to Kansas. So, to answer your question, we had told it several times before that conference.

What made you decide to start telling your story? Did you tell it one place and then other people heard about it and asked you to share?

E: We didn't say we were available to tell our story, but people knew our story and asked if we'd come and talk to them.

F: They knew it was about AIDS, and they knew the boys had died of AIDS. We were pretty open about it. A lot of people knew that part of our story. We usually didn't raise the homosexuality question unless somebody brought it up. We didn't dodge it, but we figured they wouldn't even come if we went to talk about homosexuality. So, we talked about AIDS, and we needed to do that because hundreds of people in Kansas were getting infected. We needed to make that witness.

In talking to other people about the issues of AIDS and homosexuality, some people have told me that people are much more comfortable talking about AIDS than homosexuality. Has that been your experience as well?

F: Yes, because it's a disease, but they always put the two together. If you had AIDS, you were gay. That was God's punishment.

E: People would say that to us even when we hadn't mentioned homosexuality. At the end of our talk when people were asking questions, they would ask us when we had found out our boys were gay. We hadn't even mentioned that they were gay, so it was obvious that it was assumed.

F: We don't know how much gossip went around the state while this was all going on.

What motivated you to tell your personal story, knowing it was controversial and probably being very closely scrutinized?

E: For me, I felt like it was my calling. Fritz had his call to the ministry back in the '50s, and I think I had my calling when the boys died. I really felt like this was a call. It was something that needed to be done, and who was going to do it if we didn't? We were in a position to have some influence and impact with people that others didn't have. A lay person wouldn't have the kind of influence a bishop would have. I think that's why I did it.

F: I think that was mine, too. In the election process you had the political risk. After the election, since you are elected for life, there's not much they can do to you. That reduced the risk considerably. Some people were willing to at least listen, and some were angry and hostile.

Did the idea that Jesus, a person who always loved and stood up for the underdog, so to speak, the leper in his time, encourage you to do this? Was that a way to convey his message?

F: Oh, sure. It's a justice issue. I was heavily involved in the civil rights movement, and this is a similar kind of issue. It's kind of ironic that many of the people who supported the civil rights movement don't support the movement to accept gay and lesbian people. To me, both are biblical justice issues--marching for the oppressed. To use the language of the Latin American theologian, it was a preferential option for the poor and outcasts. I guess health would be another important issue.

I remember going to one of the community forums that you two went around the state giving about the issue of homosexuality. You tried to educate and be in dialogue with the participants so that the issue was at

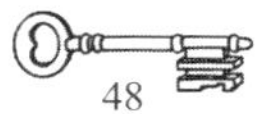

least out on the table to discuss. One person used the phrase that we hear from time to time in connection with the issue--"We can love the sinner but not the sin." Your reply was, "That doesn't feel much like love." I remember thinking that was huge. We don't always think our ideas through before we make them our framework for living our lives.

F: It feels like rejection to us, not love.

You eventually wrote a book telling your story, *Dancing in a Wheelchair: One family Faces HIV/AIDS*. It's a wonderful book with the story told in dialogue between the two of you. What prompted you to write the book?

F: Our good friend, Don Messer, former president of Iliff Seminary, had heard our story several times. He kept saying to us, "That is a story that needs to be written down and heard by many, many people. Please consider making it into a book." As we pondered the possibility, it seemed like a good idea to us as well, so we began to write.

Did you find it helpful in your faith and healing journeys?

E: Definitely. As I said before, the boys' deaths became a call to ministry for me, and the book more or less finalized that calling. As we wrote the book, we began to explore the Bible for more comfort, and also began to read other writings on the issues of death. In the process, our faith grew stronger and the healing process continued on a more intense basis.

What kind of responses did you get from people after they read your book?

We have had nothing but positive responses. We received many letters from people all over the United States, telling us how helpful it had been to them. Almost everyone told us they cried at many places in the book, feeling our pain and empathizing with us.

When we had talked earlier about the United Methodist Church slogan "Open Hearts, Open Minds, Open Doors," Fritz, you said you thought it was an encouraging thing. Do you still feel that way?

F: Etta isn't quite at the same place on that as I am. I like that language, but

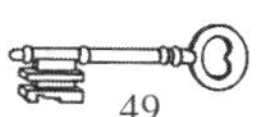

I understand why some people don't like it. I think that's who we try to be, anyway. We may not be there all the time, but I think that's who we are. We'd never say that our doors are closed, and our mission is to keep people out. We want to welcome people in, especially the outcasts. That's so much of our tradition and heritage. It gives us a challenge, anyway, to try to live up to. Hearts and minds are both part of our experience. That's the "reason and experience" parts of our Wesleyan quadrilateral. You have to get your heart right, but you also have to think right. I guess I'm still in a place that says it's a worthy thing that gives us a challenge. I have a lot of friends who say we're not there, and they can't stand the hypocrisy of that.

Is that how you feel about it, Etta Mae?

E: Yes, and listening to gay friends, I hear them say that they don't feel like the Church is really open. I guess I'm empathizing with them. On the other hand, I feel like we're struggling to be that.

It seems that it comes down to the degree of inclusion we are looking at. Some say that gays and lesbians are welcome to be in our congregations, while others want full inclusion, meaning ordination and recognition of relationships with some kind of sacred ceremony.

F: I keep saying that ought to be our goal. We need to keep moving in that direction--to find our way to the steps to get there. The Church moves slowly. We have hundreds, if not thousands of years of history to deal with. We just have a lot to overcome.

How, then, do you see the future? Do you think the Church will ever arrive at full acceptance of the issue?

F: Not in my lifetime, but it's still a life goal. You go to General Conference, and it is so negative. You get more restrictive votes every four years. I think that's because the conservatives get more and more organized, and they get more delegates in attendance. It starts in the local Annual Conferences, and the conservatives try to keep anyone with a more liberal point of view from getting elected to be a delegate to General Conference, so you get more conservative votes. The thing is, we don't get that in the local churches. Local churches are a lot more open than the General Conference is, but local churches don't write the Discipline. That's been my experience. You go to a local church Sunday school class, and of course you get some negative, judgmental stuff, but you also talk to people who are more open. When I was at Blue Springs, there was a gay couple in the community. They weren't related to the church, but one of the members called and said that there had been a death in the family, and they were afraid no pastor would work with them. She asked me if I'd go visit with them, and if I'd do the funeral. The gay couple asked if she really thought I'd come. She said, "Oh yeah, he'll come. We love everybody." And this particular lay person really did.

E: You know, I think about a little country church that had an organist who was gay, and he brought his partner to church. This was a congregation of about thirty people and they just loved those two guys. In another small church they had a gay couple in the congregation, and they were well accepted. That's where people need to go to learn about acceptance.

F: It's putting a face on the issue that makes the difference. That's another reason we wanted to tell our story to congregations, because that was a face-to-face encounter. It made people deal with us personally. It's a lot harder to attack someone face-to-face.

E: Oh, there were a few that didn't have any trouble attacking us.

F: Maybe for the hardliners, but not for most people.

E: Actually, when we went to tell our story about AIDS, we didn't encounter problems. It was when Fritz took a stand at General Conference to change the Discipline and stop discrimination against gay and lesbian people that he began to be attacked. I can think of two different churches that asked him to come and speak, and then attacked him.

Fritz, you were active at the General Conference level on this issue. Talk about the Denver Fifteen and what that was.

F: We knew that at the 1996 General Conference, we would be dealing with the closed policies in the Discipline concerning homosexuals in the Church. Some wanted to open up the policies, take out the restrictive language and go back to what we used to say, which was to say nothing. At least that was more open. Some of us bishops got to talking and said we needed to figure out a way to speak about that. Bishops can't speak on the floor of the Conference. So, some of us wrote a statement that said we called on the General Conference to be compassionate. It read like this:

We the undersigned bishops wish to affirm the commitment made at the consecration to the vows to uphold the Discipline of the church. However, we must confess the pain we feel over our personal convictions that are contradicted by the proscriptions in the Discipline against gay and lesbian persons within our church and within ordained and diaconal ministers. Those sections are paragraph 71F (last paragraph); 402.2; 906; 12 and footnote, p 205. We believe it is time to break the silence and state where we are on this issue that is hurting and silencing countless faithful Christians. We will continue our responsibility to the order and discipline of the church but urge our United Methodist Churches to open the doors in gracious hospitality to all our brothers and sisters in faith.

F: We decided we'd just release it to the press. We talked among our friends and got fifteen bishops to sign the letter. About a third of them were retired bishops.

E: The press he mentioned was the daily paper that came out of General Conference, not the regular press.

F: Well, the bishops got all excited and they hauled us in and wanted to know why we had done this. We told them that if we had brought this to the Council of Bishops, they wouldn't have let us do it, and we thought we needed to make this statement. A lot of the bishops were really angry with us--some because we hadn't processed it through them, and that we owed them that. That might have been a legitimate point. It was a huge controversy. I guess you'd say there was some fallout from it. We all paid a price for it, but I think it was the right thing to do as kind of a prophetic witness. I probably got as many letters saying they agreed with us and supported us than those who disagreed. Some letters said I ought to resign. "Leave the Church if you can't support it." I probably got about three thousand letters. I answered every letter that came to me from Kansas. The conservatives organized people, so I got a lot of these duplicated letters that people signed and sent that didn't really mean anything.

E: Kind of an update on that at the last General Conference in 2004, they had a parade--not a demonstration--of gays and lesbians and supporters who walked around the floor of the business meeting. Some people weren't comfortable walking with them, but they stood up. This time there were twenty-nine bishops standing, as opposed to fifteen. That's a very encouraging sign that the bishops are beginning to see that this is an issue that's not going to go away. That also gives some support to the gay and lesbian community.

F: The bishops who were chairs of all the General Conferences did a terrific job of presiding over the Conference and allowed the expression of opposition to take place. That was helpful.

Do you think having this issue as a personal part of your lives has made your lives or faith journeys any different? Has it added to or taken anything away from that?

E: It has affected me tremendously. The thing it has done for me is to strengthen my faith. It's much stronger than it was before. I had experienced a pretty mediocre faith before, because nothing had challenged it. The homosexuality issue, as well as the AIDS issue, challenged it. I had to deal with the illness and death of two sons. I was amazed by how strong I became through that. I would not have thought that I had that strength in me.

F: She really has grown through it all. She is even more willing than I am to take risks in the public arena, partly because of my position. I have to have some restraints. It has, of course changed my life, too. It is one thing to support inclusion of all. It's another to have it in your own family! Then you have to deal with it in a different way. I've never liked the confrontational thing, like we had in Denver. With Civil Rights I didn't go to Selma or get in the picket lines. I was always in-between, trying to build bridges. That's the way I've approached the issue of homosexuality, too. I just try to get dialogue going and build bridges. I do find it's pretty hard to do around biblical issues. I've always thought of myself as a social liberal but more orthodox on scriptural understandings and theological positions. I guess I think of myself being a moderate--at least not a "flaming" liberal. I find that you can't have very meaningful dialogue about Scripture--the authority of the Scripture. If people believe the Scriptures are dictated by God and recorded by some human beings, you can't have dialogue about that. Interpretation and all the modern scholarship just hits deaf ears. We had this dialogue in Nashville at the Commission on Christian Unity, and it wasn't very satisfying. We didn't really come up with anything. That's the case with most social issues. You write position papers, but they don't really change anything. Everybody went away thinking the same thing they thought when they came. The only way you get change is to deal with the people face-to-face. It's the same thing with nuclear weapons. You can't deal with that without talking to someone from Japan who went through the nuclear bombs.

The bottom line on the face-to-face method is that Jesus did it all the time. He was always right there with people in their daily lives.

F: I agree, but before we leave this area, I want to talk about one other thing we did at the Commission on Christian Unity. We had a dialogue up in Chicago, and we invited six people to come tell their stories. They had all left the United Methodist Church. Some had left because we were too conservative. Others left because we were too liberal. They told their stories, and you listened. You had to pay attention to the people who were there. It was such a powerful experience for us. We need to do more of that.

Do you have scriptures that are meaningful to you, that sustain you or define your faith journey?

F: I'd have to take categories of Scripture--the doctrine of grace, for example. You're saved by grace, not by the works you do or being any particular kind of person, but because God's grace is sufficient to deliver us. That would be key for me.

E: Mine is always Isaiah 40: "Mount up with wings as eagles; they shall run and not be weary; and they shall walk, and not faint." It's about knowing that God is giving me strength no matter what I do. God is always there, always has been and always will be.

F: Then there's that passage in Luke where Jesus says, "Fear not, little children: for it's God's good pleasure to give you the Kingdom." There's that grace again. It can all be summed up with God's grace.

Jerry and Maudell

Delegates for Diversity

After Cleaning Closets *came out, a member of my congregation came to me and said that she had a nephew who was gay and that her family was totally in support of him, his partner and her brother and sister-in-law. She said they were from Texas and would be coming to Kansas for a visit. She wanted to get my husband, Dale, and me together with them for a visit while they were in town. We set up a time for coffee and dessert at Jodi and Jim's house and met on Sunday afternoon. We met her brother, Jerry, and his wife, Maudell, and found them to be a delightful couple with whom we had a lot in common.*

Little did I know that years later I would get a timely call from Jerry asking me if I would consider taking on the position of the Kansas West Conference Reconciling Parents' Coordinator. I normally wouldn't have looked at a position on the Conference level, but circumstances were such that I had been feeling God's nudging me to take on something new in my justice journey connected with the Church. I didn't like the resistance I was experiencing in the Church regarding full inclusion of gay and lesbian Christians. I said I would do it.

As I got to know Jerry better through our mutual involvement, I found him to be dedicated and energetic in his quest to make positive changes in the denominational policies that were exclusionary of GLBT Christians. He and Maudell are tireless and inspirational in their efforts to gain love, acceptance and inclusion of these persons in every area of the Church.

Jerry, tell me about your growing up in the church.

Jerry: I was a Methodist. We went to a Methodist Church in a little town in Missouri. Mom was the one who saw to it that we went to church. Dad wasn't really very interested because he grew up in a home where he was taught that if he didn't accept the Bible literally he couldn't really be a Christian. He did go to a Methodist minister in town and talked to him about that. And he said,

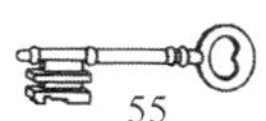

"I see a lot of people who are getting a lot out of their religious activities and I wonder if I'm missing something." The preacher he questioned very wisely gave him some books to read, as Dad was a big reader. He read those books and found out that some of the great theologians and biblical scholars and religious leaders in the world had had some of the same doubts that he did. He eventually became very active in the church and became a Methodist minister when he was about fifty or fifty-one, something like that. His first "full-time" appointment was when I was a senior in college. With his influence, I was relatively liberal in my thinking--theologically liberal. He was active in church leadership by the time I was old enough to be involved in MYF and sing in the choir and all that.

After that I went to a United Methodist college, Central Methodist College in Fayette, Missouri. That's where Maudell and I met. At that school they had a required religion course which was not really aimed at proselytizing or anything like that. It was a very informative course which came at just the right time for me, as Dad was going through what he was going through. The discussions we had about the Bible and the Christian faith fit right into the scholarly approach that the professor used in that religion course. By the time I finished all of that I was very open and liberal in my thinking but homosexuality was never mentioned. I grew up telling queer stories and I just accepted the conventional wisdom that homosexuals had to be some kind of weirdo perverts, sissies and so on. That's just what everybody thought, and that's what all of those jokes promoted.

I did have this experience that might have been important. Not only was I generally open in issues of inclusion, like race and culture, but I was a musician. I was a music major and I discovered in college, not in high school but in college, that there were people who thought that men who were musicians were queers. If not queers, at least they were sissies. If they were real men, they wouldn't be messing around with the arts, anyway. So, I had a little experience of what that was like on the other side of the issue. Now, don't misunderstand me, I don't compare that with what a gay person has to go through, but I did see a little of that. Then, when I started teaching music, I saw the effect of that on some of my students. They were harassed because they were in the band instead of playing football. It didn't happen to me as a kid, because I played football and basketball and everything else. It was a little town and everybody did everything. Anyway, I did see some of that. So all of those experiences--my liberal theology background, my experience in seeing unfair and unjust treatment of people on the basis of some characteristic like being black or being Hispanic or a musician or something like that--were important in my thinking and actions.

Maudell, do you want to add your personal experience in growing up in the church?

Maudell: I grew up in the Baptist Church, and I was from Missouri. My dad and all of his family were very strong Baptists. My mother was a Methodist, but when she married my dad, she became a Baptist. I met Jerry when I went to Central College for music--it was a good music school. I think my parents wondered at the time if that was a good idea for me to go to a Methodist school, maybe I should have gone to a Baptist school. We married and wanted to get it settled which church we were going to go to. I thought we should go to the Baptist Church, and Jerry thought we should go to the Methodist Church. We finally got that settled when we were living in Justin, because we liked the Methodist minister so well, so we started going there. Well, my dad was not happy about that but it got all right. The Baptist minister there said it didn't make any difference, just so we went to the same church, which I thought was pretty good coming from a Baptist minister.

The subject of homosexuality never came up when I was growing up and it didn't until we began to think that Chris might be gay. I remember saying to him after we had had a talk one night, I went back into his room and said, "Chris, I'd rather you'd be macho than gay." I just didn't know anything about it.

That being said, lets talk about how you found out that Chris was gay.

J: Well, I began to suspect that maybe Chris was gay, although I don't know what language I really used in thinking about it. I just noticed that he wasn't romantically interested in girls, at all. He never had any interest in a date with a girl, just to take her to a movie or to drink a Coke, or something like that. That was so different from me. I was real interested in having dates when I was growing up. Now, he had "dates" and this is a story I've heard from many, many parents with gay kids. He was very popular, president of his senior class, was an outstanding gymnast, had lots and lots of good friends. His date for homecoming his senior year was the homecoming queen, so he went out with the popular girls and all that, but they were all for special events. He didn't date just because he was interested in dating. I even told Maudell, "This isn't quite right." Her attitude about it was that the right girl just hadn't come along. We just kept at that level until he was in college. He went with the same girl, Donna, all the time he was in college. As long as he had a girlfriend, he didn't have to explain anything.

M: He even said that he and Donna were going to get married. Well, we know now that was a cover up.

J: It was a cover up to himself. He kept working to try to prove that he was not gay, even though he said that from the time he was in elementary school he had that understanding, but he was bound and determined that he was not going to do that. So, finally, we began to talk about it. I guess he was in college when we first began to talk. He always said, "No, no, I'm not." But there were just little "symptoms" that made us wonder. He finally came out to us after he graduated from college, from Texas A&M. He went to New York City to go to the American Music and Dramatic Academy. When he came home at Christmas time, I said, "Do you want to talk about your sexuality? Where do you stand on that now?" He said, "Do you want to talk about it?" I said, "If you want to talk about it." He said, "Well, I am not straight." He couldn't say, "I'm gay," only, "I am not straight."

Was this when you found out, as well, Maudell?

M: Yes, and that's when I said I'd rather he'd be macho than gay.

Did you have second thoughts after you made that comment?

M: Of course I have come a long way since then. I just didn't know that much about homosexuality, and Chris then led us along faster than we were ready to go. I remember the first Christmas after he went to New York, he was coming home, and he wanted to bring Wesley with him. We said no, that we weren't ready for that, so he came by himself. But then after that, we decided that Wesley was welcome here, too.

Do you remember what your hesitation was? Was it on religious grounds, or were you concerned about his safety, or was it the fact that you didn't know very much about it?

M: Well, we were concerned for his safety. In New York City, Chris and Wesley had been to a club, and they were on their way home, and some boys came out from the corner and started beating up on them and hitting them over the head and pulling their shirts off. So, we worried about that a lot.

What year was this?

J: That was probably in the late '80s or early '90s, somewhere in there. It's been about sixteen years.

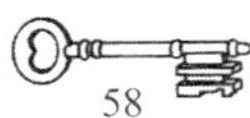

So, Chris and Wesley are still together?

M: Oh yes. They've been together, let's see, about thirteen years. They call May eigth their anniversary.

J: You know, I think both Maudell and I had the same feeling. I was probably a little farther along to acceptance than she was, but we both took the same path. I don't think our reaction to it was based on sinfulness, whether it was sinful or not. That's not the kind of theology that fits my general thinking, anyway. I think it was just the social stigma, for me, more than anything else. It was all kind of new, at least to us, in society's thinking. Many people today who have a gay child have probably thought through that, or at least many people have. Even though we had some early indications, we still thought it would be okay if the right girl came along.

Were you able to share with family at all?

M: Jerry's family knew it. Jerry told his sister and her husband, and it was just fine with them. They all accepted it. My family, being Baptists, were against it. I knew they would be. I have a younger brother who lives here and I have an older brother who lives in Missouri. One year Chris and Wesley were coming home for Christmas, and I knew that they would be around my brother and his wife, so I had to tell them. One night we had them come out and eat with us, along with their son and his wife, and we told them about it. My brother wasn't very accepting, but his wife was. She said, "This is going to be all right." And then their son just took up for Chris--he really did! He said, "There is nothing wrong with that at all." And his wife agreed with him.

The rest of my family didn't know, particularly my brother in Huntsville. Just this last Christmas, when we went up there, I had decided it was time to tell them. We were together one evening, my younger brother and my older brother, his wife, and Jerry and I said, "Chris is gay." My older brother just nodded his head as if he knew, and it was okay. My sister-in-law just kind of sat there. She didn't say anything.

Then we had a cousins' reunion. I have nine boy cousins, and I'm the only girl. We have a get together every three years. We did that this last year. All the cousins got in this room, and we started telling things about our families. When it got to me, I'd been thinking, "Am I going to tell them, or am I not? It would just be so much easier not to." But when it got to me, I just said, "Okay, I have something to tell you about Chris. Chris is gay." And they all said, "Well, that's all right. We know it." And they all knew, and it was just fine. I told them that Chris had never come to any of the reunions because I didn't know how they would treat him. They all said, "He must come. We want him to come. We want to get to know him better." I feel good now that they all know about it.

Jerry, did you have any further comments about telling family?

J: Just the nature of my family--my sister was very accepting right off the bat. Of course, there is always a little tinge of wonder as to how they're going to react before you tell them. There really wasn't much doubt in my mind but that they would accept it, and they did. Chris and Wesley have come to family reunions in Kansas and California, and everybody loves them. They have so many friends who don't have family support, and for them to be able to go to the reunions or any place in the family and be welcome is really important. So many gay and lesbian people have no place to go, and for those who do, it's like an oasis in the middle of the desert.

Do you find that the extended family has benefited from their personal experience with the issue in your family? Does it help them be more accepting of other families and perhaps even be advocates on some level?

J: To me, the "closet" is the greatest enemy we have. It's such a negative experience when they have to stay in there and hide. I understand why they have to do that. I'm not being critical, but, it's very, very costly. For the rest of us, too, the more people who can come out, the more we can put a face with this, and the easier it is for everyone. That's the value of parents' work, too.

Why don't you go ahead and talk about your activity in the Parents' Reconciling Movement.

J: I'll try to keep it brief. It's hard for me to do. As you know, the Reconciling Congregations program was what really started the movement. Well, that's not true. Affirmation was really the beginning of the program. Affirmation was the original United Methodist organization made up at that time of exclusively gay and lesbian United Methodists. There were no straight people involved in that original organization. Now they have straight allies. Out of Affirmation came the Reconciling Congregations program, which was an attempt to get congregations to adopt non-discrimination statements saying that they were open to all people.

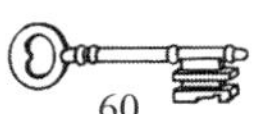

It was a little more complex than that but that came from the beginning idea. I got involved in the early '90s, prior to the Denver General Conference. That's the first I knew of the Reconciling Congregations Program. We intended to go to Denver and have the "Open the Doors" campaign--to open the doors to the members attending the General Conference and talk about the importance of open doors in the Church. Matter of fact, there are a lot of people who remember that "Open Doors" slogan in the Reconciling Congregations Program. We find it kind of ironic that the church would adopt "Open Hearts, Open Minds, Open Doors" as its slogan after that was our theme for that '96 Conference. Following that Conference, I wasn't really very active until I found out that there was a Reconciling group formed specifically for parents. I always thought that in the early days of the Reconciling movement, lay people didn't have much of a role. That was perhaps a misconception. I felt that they needed to have a bigger role to help the clergy in the task. When I saw the parents who were going to be a big part of the lay involvement, then I got very interested. It was then that I agreed to become the parent coordinator for the Central Texas Conference. Then I was invited to go to Chicago to be a member of the steering committee for the Parents' Reconciling Network. I agreed at that time to become the jurisdictional coordinator and finally the facilitator of the steering committee.

Maudell, have you served in any official capacity in any of these areas, or are you in more of a support role?

M: I have served more in a support role. I'm not as active in it as Jerry is. We have a support group at our church, and I'm involved in that. It's not that I'm against it. I'm just not as active as Jerry is.

Have you found that it is more difficult to find acceptance and support, being in the "conservative South?"

M: I don't think it's any more of an issue, for me, here.

J: It's no issue for me personally. I would feel the way I feel no matter where I lived. What I find is that there is a perception that there is a greater conservatism in all subjects. I think if you look at it as red states-blue states, then it's true. You can't deny the statistics there. Certainly, if you look at the Pacific Northwest Conference and some of the Conferences in the Northeast, you'll see a difference. However, I also know that there are some areas of the country, for instance in California, where we certainly have wonderful leadership, but the California

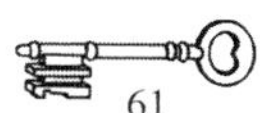

Pacific Conference is still split about fifty-fifty on this issue. I guess that's a longwinded answer to your question. The real answer is, "Yes, I know there's more resistance, or at least less openness, in the South. It is better in metropolitan cities than in rural areas."

Do either of you have favorite scriptures that encourage you or help you oppose negative encounters on this subject?

J: I don't have specific scriptures that I can quote to somebody, but I think if you look at the overriding message of the Scriptures, it is a message of inclusiveness and love, compassion, mercy, and all those positive things without all the judgment. It has little to do with sexual rules and regulations. It's based upon principles of love and inclusion. Bill McElvaney, who was at Perkins School of Theology talked recently about Christian tradition and the Christian Right. He says they have completely confused the issue. The Christian tradition is based upon Christ. I can't state it nearly as eloquently as he did, but the point he was making is that if you look at the Christian tradition, the way Christ lived, it's not what the Religious Right is saying at all. It is the complete opposite of that. So, if you want to return to the Christian tradition, you can't do what they are saying. It would be exclusionary and mean-spirited. I think the testimony of the Scriptures as a whole, not specifically those parts used against gays and lesbians, is important. If you understand what those scriptures really mean it makes a difference, too. I use a Walter Wink publication, *Homosexuality and the Bible*, I believe it's called. What he says is that the Bible did not include sexual mores. He says it does have rules and regulations, some of which we accept today, and some which we reject. In other words, we still wouldn't think prostitution is okay, but the Bible included concubines and the marrying of one's brother's spouse. We reject those things and accept some other things. He says it has a love ethic which we are to apply to all things.

When you hear the slogan "Open Hearts, Open Minds, Open Doors," what comes to mind for you?

J: Sometimes I kind of laugh about it, and other times I get angry about it. I think it's a slogan that reveals the blindness of the Church. They really think the doors should be open, and they think they are open. What they're saying is that we want more people to come to our church. It's an evangelist slogan, I guess. They just don't realize how offensive that slogan is to those people to whom the doors are closed, and hearts and minds are closed. It seems to me to be very deceptive. The people who are deceived the most are the leadership of the Church. The more I dwell on it, I guess, the angrier I get.

Some have said that they feel like it is a challenge to the Church and that it will grow into it. Do you think that is a possibility?

J: Sure, I think that's a possibility, but I'm not sure that the people that came up with that slogan saw it that way. That isn't why they came up with that slogan. They weren't trying to play into the sexual orientation issue at all. I don't think if there would have been a gay person on the committee, they would ever have adopted that. People who don't deal with this on a personal basis don't understand the impact that the slogan has.

We used it at our Reconciling event at the end of April. We asked Bill McElvaney if he would come and speak on what is the real meaning, the true theological meaning, of "Open Minds, Hearts, and Doors." He did a wonderful, wonderful job. So, yes, I think it is something we could use. I don't think it was mean-spirited, I really don't. I don't think the people who designed that did it with anything other than good intentions, but it's just another indication of the blindness toward this issue.

One of the things I'm looking at is what influence being involved with the gay community, spiritually as well as socially, might have had on your spiritual journey. What are your thoughts on that?

J: Well, I think the key there is "journey." One of my favorite quotes is the one that says, "Follow those who seek the truth, but doubt those who find it." That says to me that you always need to be gleaning your mind for the possibility that there's something out there that you thought you were sure of, and that you might find out you were wrong about. New information and new experiences lead us in new directions, and God is at work in that. Some people are saying, "Why can't you accept the possibility that God is doing a new thing with sexual orientation," and I do believe God does this with us all the time. He does open doors. I guess it's just another step in my own ability to accept people who are different than I am. One of my big challenges, one that I still struggle with, is people who are on the other end of this spectrum. I just have a difficult time with it. It's a test--it really is a test, isn't it? If I'm mean-spirited then how can I accuse them of being mean-spirited? That's my challenge. I have to find ways to deal with that. I work at it, but it is a journey.

I think this experience is a step forward in the wonderful diversity of God's creation. I had a woman in a Sunday school class I was teaching say that diversity is divisive. There is a concept out there today that claims diversity is bad, and that's wrong. God's creation is wonderfully diverse. Diversity is what gives life and depth and meaning and strength. It's true for this country, so why wouldn't it be true for the church? Diversity is something we ought to welcome and encourage. So, I guess I'd say a greater appreciation for diversity in God's creation is a part of my growth.

Are you hopeful that the Church will someday be balanced and embrace full inclusion of gays and lesbians in the life of that institution?

M: Oh, I don't know. Our church, I think, has come a long way, but as far as all churches, I don't know. I think it's going to take a long time.

J: I think that we'll change the rules in the United Methodist Church. I think we'll see some moderation. I don't know what it will be, but I think we'll see some moderation in the negative statements in 2008. What you have to understand, I believe, is that this issue is not the issue. It' a symptom of the issue. The real issue has to do with the power struggle that's going on theologically in the Church. It's about whether or not the conservative view of scripture has more authority than the liberal view of scripture. It's about the conflict between emphasizing social justice or personal salvation. To tell you the truth, I think religion is being used by political forces which are trying to change our culture. So, I think we're going to change the rules, I really do. We're not going to just throw aside the whole Discipline, but I do think we'll move in the direction of moderating it. Then, however, we have the same kind of future to deal with that we've had with racism. We're still seeing it today--the Senate voted to make apologies for the fact that we didn't stand up and pass laws against lynching. Isn't that amazing that this is 2005, and they're just getting around to doing that? We made apologies from the United Methodist Church in Pittsburgh at the 2004 General Conference in a service where they apologized, officially to the Black churches for the way they were treated in our Denominations' history. One of these days we're going to have to do the same thing about the way we've treated sexual minorities. So, I think we'll change the rules, but as far as changing all the hearts, it's not going to happen any more than it's happened with race. I will say, though, that what I have come to feel about that is that it's not my problem. All I can do is to deal with my

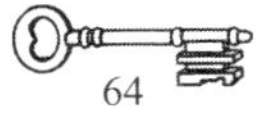

own circle, and I'll do everything that I can. If we can move a little bit at a time, then that's what we have to do. You sort of have to leave the rest of it to God, and in God's time it will be taken care of.

Do either of you have any additional comments you want to make?

J: I talked a little bit about the importance of coming out of the closet a little earlier. I think that is so important. Your first book, *Cleaning Closets* was published, and I think it was helpful, whether you are a parent or someone who doesn't have a gay child or relative, to stand up and let it be known that you do believe that discrimination on the basis of sexual orientation or gender identity is wrong. When people see that Maudell and I are open about this, and that we have a gay son we accept and who's welcome in our home--that we treat him with love and respect--what they see is helpful. They start to think, "We've known Jerry and Maudell for a long time and have seen Chris grow up and they aren't some kind of weirdo perverts, so maybe there's something here we ought to know about." I think it's valuable to put a face on the issue. It stops being a theological or a cultural issue and becomes a very personal one. That's the only way we'll ever really solve this issue. When it's somebody they know who is being hurt by their discrimination that puts it on a whole different level.

M: I was going to say that Jerry was teaching a lot of Sunday school classes on social principles, and he told every class he taught that our son, Chris, was gay. One man in one of the classes said, "That took an awful lot of courage for you to say that." We think that he probably doesn't go along with it, but everybody else accepted it, and it's okay. We feel good about letting people know that Chris is gay.

Chuck

The Gift

I need to introduce Chuck and Brian W. together, even though they are not a romantic couple and will be interviewed separately, so they can tell their stories individually. When I was talking to them at the installation of our Conference bishop, some months before I started the interviewing process, Brian defined their relationship as non-conventional. I didn't ask any questions at the time, but it was the first thing I asked him when I arrived at their home after church on a Sunday afternoon in the following February.

Chuck was dressed in his bathrobe, as he was recovering from surgery. The surgery was to have been a simple procedure, but had been more serious than first thought. Brian had taken the week off from work to take care of Chuck. The smell of brownies filled the air and suggested that we might experience an extra measure of hospitality with refreshments.

I asked Brian what a "non-conventional" couple was. He said that because he and Chuck had lived as roommates for a number of years and were often seen together at church and other meetings, people assumed that they were romantically involved. Brian said he had explained on numerous occasions that they were just good friends. However, many people seemed to be unconvinced that their relationship was only friendship. Chuck told me he'd given up and let those people assume whatever they wanted to.

Brian is in his late forties and Chuck is a number of years older. Brian works in the medical community doing grant work, and Chuck is a retired United Methodist minister. Both are involved and committed to justice issues and Reconciling Ministries. Their personalities, styles of ministry, and stories are unique and distinct from each other.

Let's start by exploring your religious roots, talking about your spiritual foundation.

Chuck: Well, I was born in Sycamore, down by Independence, Kansas, and it was during the Depression, so after a few months my father moved us to Michigan where there was a lot of work. My first fourteen years were lived there, and it was during that time that I began to become aware of who I was. It just wasn't acceptable in society at that time to be gay, so it was just something within me--I didn't tell anyone or talk about it. I had no one to talk to.

After I moved back to Montgomery County, where home was, where I was born, and went to school in Independence, I knew for sure what my orientation was, but at the time there were lots of reasons not to say anything. Churches didn't say anything about sex in the forties, but it was just kind of there. You knew what the Church felt without the Church saying it. I knew that society felt that it was a mental illness, and if you said you were gay, or whatever term you used, you would be put in a mental institution, and they would use shock therapy and various things. I think the social pressure was more of a pressure on me than the stigma of mental illness. I just never felt ill.

I dated girls because I knew that was what I was supposed to do. I still had my feelings, but there was no one to talk to about them. Then I went to college. My feelings were still there. It's kind of interesting--all through high school, my closest friend and I were in band and drama together. He went off to college one way, and I went off to college another way. At our forty-fifth class reunion--forty-five years after we graduated from high school--we were both back for the reunion, and after breakfast one morning during the three day reunion he said, "I want to talk to you," and I said, "Okay. I want to talk to you, too."

I had decided that since he was my closest high school friend and he knew nothing about my orientation, and I knew nothing about his, I was going to tell him. If he didn't want to be friends, that was his choice. We sat down and started visiting, and the first thing he said to me was, "You know, I'm gay." I said, "I can't believe it--so am I."

The same thing happened to me in college. My roommate, Arthur, who was from Colorado, a Hispanic guy and a good friend, went home with me for Easter vacation--he and another friend. Then, about thirty years after we had graduated, a friend and I decided we wanted to go to California and visit Arthur. He had called and wanted us to come out, but he said, "I need to tell you before you come, you might not want to come--I am gay." So, they were two of my closest friends, one from high school and one from college, and we did not know each other's orientations. It was that much in the closet.

When did you begin to sense your call to the ministry?

I really wanted to go to seminary. I wanted to be a pastor--also wanted to be a school teacher. I got to seminary. My last year of college on a choir tour, I met a girl, my roommate's cousin. She was a Spanish girl. I started writing to her, and I thought I was in love. I thought this would prove something. She's Catholic and Spanish--this will be a social witness or whatever. I was at seminary one year, and then she and I got married. I'd only seen her, I think, three times, and I came back to Sycamore and got married. Well, it was a bad choice from the beginning. First of all, I didn't really know how to relate to a woman--certainly didn't have the skills to understand anything. The marriage didn't last long. We separated, and she moved to New York City. We got a divorce.

I talked to one of my seminary professors about my orientation and he said, "You will overcome it. It's something you can deal with. You just go ahead and be a pastor and this will pass."

Well, it was about that time that one of my co-workers wanted me to go on a date with a friend of his. I knew from hearing conversations that she was dating a guy that I knew, and he was gay. She also knew he was gay, so, maybe she would be accepting. I went on the date and eventually, we got married, but I didn't share who I was.

The struggle with feeling a sense of guilt and not being accepted by God was even stronger than the sense of guilt for not being who I was any other time. I would work hard, thinking that if I were a successful pastor, then God would overlook my problem, or maybe I wouldn't be judged too badly, and he would somehow accept me. The theology of this, well, its bad theology, but it's very emotional. I was appointed to serve one church and then another and then a third, so I only served three churches in thirty-one years.

When I came to St. Paul's Church, I worked very hard. It was a church that needed a lot of support. We did a lot of work with the inner city--really creative things. I worked day and night at the church. Of course, that didn't make it easy for the person who followed me, but that was who I was, and they just had to be whoever they were. I still struggled with my feelings. I never, ever, ever dated anyone on the side in all this period of time. If I were ever with anyone, I didn't want it to be emotional or physical--I just couldn't handle that.

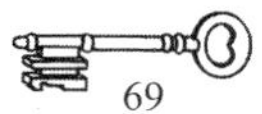

You were still married at this time, correct?

Oh, yes, still married. I went on a trip with St. Paul's Church to New Mexico. I did it several different times as a way of experiencing the culture and visiting McCurdy School--getting acquainted with a whole different world. In fact, I took several trips to various places around the world with people from St. Mark's to help myself experience the wider world. We always planned to be there from the middle of one week to middle of the next week, so we could be in Santa Fe over the week-end and could go to a Spanish mass, then to St. John's United Methodist Church. On one particular trip, in May of 1985, I met an artist one Saturday evening, and we started talking. He was younger than I was, and I really liked him a lot. We talked a lot about who he was and who I was. He was from Paris, and at that time he was about thirty. He told me his story.

When he was about nineteen, he was having an affair with a young man in Paris, and his father found out about it, not who it was, but just found out about his being gay. He told him all kinds of negative things--that God hated him, and he was going to hell--all the things people say. Then he called the parish priest over to reinforce all the things he was saying. The young priest reinforced all the things the father had said.

Phillip said. "I just couldn't handle it. I had to leave, because the priest was the one that I'd had the affair with." He got on a boat to New York City, where he'd studied for a while, and then he came to Santa Fe to work. As far as I know, he's still in Santa Fe.

I asked him if he'd ever gone back to church in the last ten years.

"I didn't go back until last Christmas Eve. I went to mass for the first time in ten years, and I was sitting in mass and thought, 'I don't need a priest to tell me I'm okay,' and I went down for communion."

So the next Sunday on the week-end of May 19th, our group was in church at eight o'clock. Of course, it was in Spanish, so I didn't understand much of what was being said, but I was there, and I kept thinking about what Phillip had said. During the first forty-five minutes of the service, I just had kind of an epiphany experience that I was acceptable as I was, and that I didn't have to be any different. It was okay. I started to cry--tears were running down on my shirt. The poor people from St. Paul's didn't know what was going on. Probably thought I was losing it, and I was losing it. When it was time for communion I just got up and went down. The priest doesn't know I'm a Methodist pastor, doesn't know I'm gay. He'll serve me communion, which he did. I've been back to that church a number of times, and I can walk right back to the pew where I was sitting.

When I got home, things kind of fell into place--I was just a different person. I started to do a lot of writing for the church on devotions. When I retired, the church put many of these devotions into a publication. I just became more effective.

What was going on at home with your family life while all these changes were taking place? Do you think that your rocky family life was part of the reason you were working so hard?

I'm sure it was. The family life began to deteriorate more and more, to the point that I was almost never home. The last years before I retired, I never ate any meals at home--I slept there, and that was about it.

Were there children, by now?

There were children. Karen was born in '60, so she was twenty-five--she was out on her own. Mike was born in '65, and he had moved to Colorado after he got out of high school to work, so he wasn't at the house much. Our relationship just didn't exist, at this point. Margaret had her life, and I had mine. She had quit going to church.

Do you think she knew or suspected why?

She just knew that there wasn't a good relationship. Two or three things happened that year that were really significant. Long about the first of June, one of the church members said that his older brother was coming home from Philadelphia to die--he had AIDS. In 1985, it was almost non-existent in Wichita. Nobody knew how to deal with it. I asked him if I could tell the congregation the next Sunday, and he agreed. So, in the middle of the service, I just said that Kevin would be coming home from Philadelphia to live--that he was dying of AIDS, and we had a prayer for him. He did come home, but the groundwork had been laid. He became active in the church, and in 1986 we had the first educational seminar on AIDS for family members and social workers, doctors, clergy, and a lot of people came. Dr. Sweet came and spoke. It was the first time she spoke publicly about AIDS. It was in conjunction with the county health department, so we had a lot of resources to do the seminar. Kevin lived until a year and a half after that seminar. He was active in the church until he died.

Was he well accepted?

He would help fix covered dish dinners and work in the kitchen, and no one thought anything about it. Everyone just treated him as being sick, not as being contagious. It was just amazing. They were supportive of him. If I hadn't felt okay about myself, I wouldn't have felt good about doing that. The interesting thing about the seminar--there was only one cleric who came, and he was a priest from Andover. No other Catholic or Protestant clergy came. We had quite a few people from the congregation who came, a lot of nurses and social workers. There were sisters, too. We had a lot of sisters who came to me from Newman University asking us to sponsor speakers whom they weren't allowed to have on their campus, like Matthew Fox. We had 360 people registered for a three-day seminar, and there was only one priest, but there were Catholics from about ten states who came to the seminar.

How long was it, then, before you left the ministry?

I was a pastor for three more years.

Was there a divorce in the middle of all this?

No, a couple of things happened. One of our soloists at the church had AIDS--he wasn't thirty yet when he died. The church loved him. He was an absolutely fantastic soloist and active in stuff all over Wichita. When he died, we had the funeral at the church--the church was filled--hundreds of people were there. We were in the process of remodeling the parking situation, so they had to walk around to the front door. Well, I was in my study and one of the morticians came in and said, "You need to be aware that Fred Phelps is picketing." It was the first funeral service he had decided to picket. I went out. At first I got so angry. This was about forty-five minutes before the service started, and I went out on the sidewalk and confronted him. By this time the police had been called, and they were already there. Everybody had to walk through the picket line to get into the church through the front door. I knew if I hit him, which I wanted to do, that I would be hauled off by the police. I was in my robe, and I just walked up to him, and I kept hitting him with my stomach and pushing him with my stomach. He screamed at the police to arrest me, because I was hitting him. I remember saying to the police that I was hitting him with my fat stomach, and if that was an assault, come and arrest me. The police kind of ignored us both, hoping we'd go away.

I went back to my study, and I figured I had to become at peace with myself--I couldn't just let this go on. Somehow, I had to not be angry when I conducted the funeral. So I went back out onto the front porch, and there was one of the members of his church videoing everybody who was coming into the church, or at least pretending to be videoing--whether she was or not, I don't know. So I said to her, "Would you come in and join us in the service?" She looked at me with strange bewilderment and said, "Oh no, I might catch AIDS!" I said to her, "Oh honey, we don't have sex during worship." I felt okay from then on. He chose to picket me for another funeral, and he picketed my retirement in 1993.

In about '90 or '91 I knew Margaret and I were just living in the same house and that we had to at least communicate or it would get really bad, so we went for counseling, to a person we both knew. We went four or five times. We talked, but we never really hit the subject. Finally, he said, in front of Margaret, "Are you gay?" I said that was an unfair question. I wanted to talk to him about it in private. I didn't know how to respond to him.

When I did talk to him at another session, I said, "I am, and I'm not ashamed of it, and I'm okay with it." He said, "You're going to have to talk to her about this." So I did.

Was she surprised?

No, that's the strange part. The interesting thing was, and I didn't know this, that she knew my first wife. My first wife was a dance teacher, and her partner was someone Margaret had dated. The three of them had been together at a party. When Margaret and I had our first date, my first wife hadn't moved to New York yet, and she told Margaret, "He's gay."

I didn't know she knew, and I didn't know she'd told Margaret. Margaret didn't believe her. So it wasn't too big a surprise when I confirmed it. So, my children and my wife became pretty distant--just non-communicative.

There was a younger person that I cared about very deeply, and we did many things together, but he never could accept the fact that he was bi-sexual. We did have this strong friendship, and we traveled together to Europe and so on. He helped me move to New Mexico, because when I retired I knew I had to be by myself. I knew I had to have a fresh start and to live as a gay man.

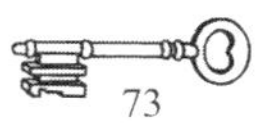

At what age did you retire?

I retired at age sixty-two, in 1993. I had decided that I was at an age that I would never have a relationship with anyone. I was going to live the rest of my life alone, and I was going to be okay with that.

By 1994, I was ready to come back to Wichita, and I decided to go back to school. I didn't worry about dating--I was okay with being by myself. Eventually, I started back to church at College Hill United Methodist Church.

Why did you choose College Hill?

I knew they were open to gay and lesbian members and had clergy support, and that it was okay. You could be out and be gay and the church was okay with that. I could go back to college and enjoy being a student, which I did. I graduated from Wichita State in '97 with a degree in German.

Are you totally retired now?

I work for a flower shop in sales. I was the pastor of the owner for eighteen years. I conducted his wedding, baptized his children, baptized his grandson, and conducted the funeral for his daughter who was killed in a car accident.

I know you preached a "coming-out" sermon at College Hill. How did that happen?

My "coming-out" sermon was after I met Brian. I had talked to Brian about it, and he had wanted to organize a worship service. In organizing the music, I wanted to use a song from the "Hunchback of Notre Dame," "God Help the Outcasts." So a soloist and professional musician sang, and then I told my story. I hadn't really wanted to say to the congregation and the whole world that I'm gay, so I'd decided to tell my story without saying the specific words. But, when I started the talk, I decided that I just had to say it as it was--I felt, in the eighth grade, before we left Michigan, that I was going to be a pastor. I knew by the time I was in the eighth grade that my sexual orientation--where I really felt attraction--was with other guys. That was my story.

Then, as I got older and started to think back, I remembered when I was young, second and third grade, in a little one-room schoolhouse. There were two girls in my class. They had a brother who was probably two or three years older than I was, and I just thought he was wonderful. I used to get permission to go over to their farm and play with my two classmates, so I could be close to Jack. One of the last trips I made to Israel, we were sitting in the airport, and there were two older ladies across from us. I got my camera out, and I took a picture of them by accident and they laughed. Then we discovered we were all going to the Holy Land on the same trip. So, I said to them, "Where are you from?" They said Beaverton, Michigan. That was a wee town near where that school was. When I asked them if they knew the Woodruff family, they said they did. I asked about Blanch and her sister and their older brother, Jack--if they knew where they were. They said it was kind of sad--Jack had committed suicide. I never got a chance to tell him how important he had been in my life--only from a distance.

So I remember those feelings, and they were very real. Even in the second and third grade, I knew who I wanted to be with.

What happened after you shared all of this with the congregation? Were they accepting and supportive?

Well, it's kind of interesting. Some people accepted it and apparently, some left the church after I talked--dropped out of College Hill. So, I guess it created kind of a stir.

There were a couple of times, when I was at St. Paul's before 1985, that I'd reached a point in my life that I didn't think I could take it any more. One time was in late summer--actually, it was November, and I decided that this was it. I was just going to commit suicide. I could not go on. The conflict was too great.

Was your conflict with being gay, or with God not accepting you?

That was the conflict. I couldn't change who I was, and I couldn't change how I thought God felt about that, because that's what the Scripture said. So, I got everything in order. I cleaned my desk. Everyone should have known that with a clean desk there was something seriously wrong, because my desk was usually so bad.

I have to tell you this. One year, during the week between Christmas and New Years, the church had been broken into. On Monday morning, when the police came into my office, they said, "My gosh, they have messed up your

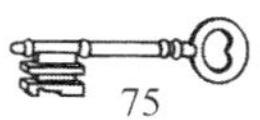

desk," and they took pictures of my desk. My secretary was in the other room just laughing to herself--bent over laughing, because my desk was just like it had been when we had left. They hadn't bothered my desk.

So, I had my desk all in order, but I decided I had to tell Margaret. I had everything prepared. I knew where the insurance papers were and so on. She said, "If you don't go to the doctor, I'm going to have you committed."

So, I went to the doctor, our family doctor, and I didn't tell him why I was depressed, just that I was depressed enough that I wanted to take my life. He said you have to go away, for at least a week, just get out and see if you can handle it. This was the first week of Advent, so, after I preached on Sunday, I used an airplane ticket to New York City. I had a gay couple in New York City that I knew. One of them I had met even before I met Margaret, and Margaret knew him, too. So, I went to stay with them. We talked a whole week. It was a great breathing time. He said, "You can make it," and by the time I flew home on Saturday, I knew I could make it.

You have talked several times about things that have happened that changed the course of your life, one way or another. In your faith journey, do you feel that those were divine interventions?

It's hard to know. I think I find purpose in how events turn out. Now, whether events come first or I find purpose in the midst of them, I'm not sure. I do know I always find purpose that I am in the right place at the right time. Many things have happened to me that I don't understand.

For instance, when I was a junior in college in Nebraska, I got to feeling really lethargic. I knew that my mother had had anemia from time to time, so I thought maybe that was my problem. I went to the college doctor, who said, after he did the blood test, "You need to go to your family doctor at home."

So I made arrangements to go on Easter vacation, and I got some blood work done. Now this was in 1952. After he got the blood work back, he called my mother and me into his office and said, "Well, you've got just three years left to live. You need to plan what you're going to do with it."

Well, my mother just came unglued, and I was kind of in a state of shock, because I didn't feel that bad. He said, "You have a disease called polycythemia. You manufacture too many red blood cells. You now have twice as many as you should have. They will soon be unable to function, and you'll starve to death, because they won't be able to carry nutrition around your system. There's no treatment for it except to take blood out. There is a doctor in Kansas City who is experimenting with radio active phosphorous. I'm going to make an appointment for you to see him."

Well, in the meantime I went back to college, but I did go to Kansas City to see the doctor. He was experimenting with radioactive phosphorus. You drink it, and it goes into your blood steam, and it kills part of the red blood cells. This was developed after 1945, so it was still in experimental stage. I took three treatments during my senior year--one in the fall, one in the winter, and one in the spring. I had planned to go to Europe right after college and work as a volunteer in the summer of '53. I asked the doctor if I should go, and he said to go.

At the end of my senior year, our college choir took a trip down to New Mexico, down to McCurdy to sing. We took a little side trip down to a place called Chimayo. Chimayo has a little church, and in their sanctuary is a place where people get dirt for healing. The church has been there since the early 1800's, and before that it was a place of healing for Native Americans. So, I went there with the class and I got a little glass of the dirt and brought it back to college with me. I still have it sitting on my dresser.

I went to seminary in Ohio, at Columbus, and the doctor there gave me another treatment of radioactive phosphorous. I kept watch of my blood count, and in 1959 I went back for one more treatment. After that my blood count was reasonably stable, a little elevated, but always the same. I don't know why it went into remission. Years later, KU Med Center had me come back for a whole series of tests to find out why I hadn't died. They had found out that the radioactive phosphorous was not a good treatment. They couldn't figure out why I went into remission. I don't know.

Now that you have found a church where you are comfortable and feel accepted, tell me how that allows you to be in ministry.

I serve on various committees at church, but of course, mission has always been my passion. From the very beginning of my life this has been my interest, and so I've raised funds for missions. In fact, Dr. Youngman and I have pushed raising funds to endow scholarships for the African University. We've raised almost $35,000 for the first endowment from the Wichita area. The reason I went to Europe was not exactly for missions, but we talked about what it was to be a peacemaker. One of the dominant thoughts is that you have to get acquainted with your enemy. In 1953, the war had only been over a short time, and the enemy was Germany. We went to live in Germany for the whole summer, and on the way over I met another person who made a very deep impact on my life. That was Andrew Young and his first wife Jean, who died of cancer. He was the first person I'd ever been friends with who was black. It just changed my whole perspective.

What do you hope to do that you haven't done yet?

I've been asked to do several talks and lectures. One university asked me to do a talk for their diversity week. I've been to your church for a diversity weekend. I've written to the congressmen from here in Kansas about the anti-gay amendment. I've been part of the Reconciling movement and sponsored several Reconciling events. I went to speak for gay rights at the General Conference in Cleveland, and I will continue to do that. I don't know that it will make a difference in my lifetime, but I just think it will make a difference, eventually

Do you think the Church will ever be reconciled?

The Church has to confront its own exclusiveness, and little by little, it is. To put it in writing is another thing. When you talk to people individually, its one thing--they don't believe there should be these rules. They think people who are gay should be allowed to be clergy. Most people at Annual Conference know I'm gay, at least those who are anti-gay, because we've talked about it in small meetings. One person told me I needed to give up my credentials. I said I wasn't going to. I told him if he wanted to bring charges, I'd understand. We'd still be friends. No one has ever brought charges, at least not to this point. I've been retired now for twelve years. If they bring charges, I'll just have to face that. Since so many people in the Conference know I'm gay, it's very important that I be active in the Conference. It gives it a face, so this is another way of promoting acceptance.

Does the theme "Open Hearts, Open Minds, Open Doors" bother you?

I think it's a goal. There are so many ways of having open minds. To be exclusive about the love of God only going to certain people, and if you're not one of those people, you don't get the love of God, isn't one of them. They may not say it that way, but that's the way it's lived out. So when you have open hearts and open minds and open doors, it's more than how the local congregation functions. It's how you function theologically and as a community. Here in Wichita, we have hundreds of people who practice different religions than we do. This really bothers some people instead of their celebrating that fact. I think the theme of the Church can be really meaningful, if that's the way it is. It's a goal.

Is there anything we haven't talked about that you want to comment on?

You know what you do does more to promote openness and sharing in a way that people can relate to. As a parent, as a church member, telling a story that people can relate to is as effective as anything anyone can do.

I also want to comment on my friendship with Brian. I met Brian in the fall of 1994, about the time I'd started college. George, our minister, had asked me to start a Sunday school class primarily for persons who were gay and lesbian. As it turned out, the class is gay, lesbian and straight. That fall, the class had only been going for a few weeks, and Brian came to Sunday school. I called him and thanked him for being there. He asked me if I wanted to go out for lunch or dinner, and I did. Then I had to go to Mexico. When I got back, we went out again to my favorite restaurant. Turns out it's not his favorite restaurant.

So, we spent time together. We went to Reconciling events together. What really kind of bonded us together was in '97, right after I had graduated, I discovered I had cancer and had to have a kidney removed. When I came home from the hospital, Brian stayed with me, because I couldn't stay by myself. Our friendship just grew from there. We went to Atlanta to a Reconciling meeting. We had a great time together, and he provided the funds for me to go.

When I had to take over the payments for Margaret's house when she could no longer work, he suggested we take an apartment together, which we did. The apartment was all right, even though it was too small for all my stuff. The main problem was that it was so noisy, so Brian suggested he buy a house, and he did. This house is his, but we share some of the expenses. I couldn't have survived financially if he hadn't helped me. And now, after surgery, again, he has taken care of me--took a week and a half off work to be a twenty-four hour nurse. He slept on the floor by my bed. He is my good friend.

I want to say something about my overall family situation now. When I returned to Wichita after spending a year in New Mexico, Margaret and I began to talk. After Brian and I began spending time together, I just said that if there were a family gathering, Brian would be there. At first, my daughter wasn't too excited about it, but now, Brian's a part of every family gathering. Margaret and Brian and I do things together a lot, because Margaret considers Brian a part of her life. If she needs something, she will call Brian and ask him for it. We have a better relationship now than we did in our whole life together. My two children have a really good relationship with Brian now, too. This last Christmas--keep in mind I'd never talked to my brother and his wife about my sexual orientation--my little brother and his wife and Margaret and Michael, my youngest son, were here for Christmas dinner, in our home. The family relationship is good. I'm very grateful for that.

Brian W.

Soul Liberty

Brian is a person with amazing energy. His tall, slender stature suggests that his metabolism works at an accelerated rate. Anything Brian takes on as a project, whether work or volunteer status gets his full commitment and attention. There is passion in his voice when he speaks of things he is excited about, and an intellect that lets you know he has facts and figures to back his passion up. His involvement in Sunday school and church activities is serious business to him as his spiritual roots reach deep. As a gay man, issues of justice and fairness have personal implications for Brian, but not exclusively in the area of homosexuality. Fairness and equality for all people are important to him. Friendship is important, as is witnessed in his long and committed friendship with his housemate, Chuck. I interviewed him in the home that they share.

Brian, did you grow up in the church or did you start going later in life?

Brian: I grew up very churched because of my parents. We grew up in an American Baptist congregation in North Wichita. That laid a lot of beliefs in place that are still there. So the proverb about "training up a child in the way he'll walk" really feels true in a lot of ways for me. I question a lot of things now, in my late forties, that I was taught to just accept as a child. I changed some of the ideas. It's paradoxical, but it still feels like I haven't really changed my fundamentals. Sometimes I feel very conservative--very Orthodox--even though the outward expression of those beliefs might appear to be the exact opposite.

Did you ever hear anything growing up in the church that was detrimental or condemning about homosexuality?

In terms of sex or relationships, there was absolutely nothing said, which was

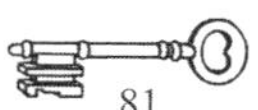

a good fit for my family, because my family didn't talk about sex. I found out much later that my parent's parents probably didn't give them any information about sex either. My background was that you had no information and there was secrecy about it. It got a negative valuation. Anything that was totally silent had to be unspeakable. Much later, I wondered how it could possibly make sense for straight people to be told that sex is terribly problematic. Then, after one brief ritual, in a one hour wedding ceremony, suddenly it's okay. I mean, how does this sudden transformation occur? It never made sense to me.

What I've seen in United Methodist Churches is that you can find some congregations that give actual attention to sex education, to relationships--those kinds of important things. I never noticed that happening in the American Baptist Church. The main message was silence, and anything that was silent was considered unspeakable, and therefore, a problem or concern. It wasn't appropriate to church conversations. There was a narrow kind of zone in which "this is religious--this is church stuff--this is what Christianity is about"--and beyond that, you were not to have an opinion.

Like, when I was a kid there was the Vietnam War. We were not to have an opinion about that. Church was about Bible, spiritual disciplines, having personal salvation in Jesus, and going to heaven. It was all about an afterlife. They prescribed certain forms of obedience and not disobeying was a sign of spirituality in this life. There was no sense of social justice, war, and those things. Those things have come to my attention now, but in my religious upbringing they were irrelevant.

What happened, then, when you started thinking that perhaps you were different? With that kind of a background, how did that affect you?

Well, I spent a lot of my energy trying to be very churchy because relationships with guys and sex were so totally problematic, period. I put all my energy into being good. I was the perfect church person. The only thing I didn't do was go out for church sports. I didn't play softball or basketball but I could lead. I could be a contributing member to any committee, any group. I could do music, I could do the Christian education, and I was even the church janitor. But in college I reached the point where I thought, "There's got to be more." I felt like I'd already mastered it. I'd already done all of the churchy things and there had to be more to God.

So there was a sort of longing?

Yeah. I did a lot of Bible studies. Now, for conservatives, I'm really bad news because I can hold my own if people start talking about the Bible. I was leading Bible studies that came out of a conservative kind of structure and tone, but in my hands they came out differently. I kind of made my way around Scripture seeking a maturity of depth and meaning, always asking more questions as I tried to put it into practice. That led me into a greater concern with relationships in small groups rather than with big structures and big systems.

When I was working on my masters at Wichita State, I was moving away from institutional church structures. I was having more and more problems with institutions which is probably a by-product of my generation. We'd already seen a lot that was suspicious in organizations--whether the military or the university. I'm very suspicious of authorities and organizations. It's paradoxical. I can be very obedient and yet, I also don't trust them.

None of this caused your faith to waiver, did it?

No, my faith, I think, was always getting stronger and more perfected. That sounds arrogant--I'm not there, but you keep learning and adjusting. That's what it was about for me. So those are my American Baptist roots, with an idea from Roger Williams who was from Providence, Rhode Island. I have "soul liberty." My liberty is completely in God and I will try to get along with any group, any church structure until push comes to shove, and I cannot follow. Then I have to part company because I have to have liberty for my soul, and it's very individualistic in the American Baptist tradition. Southern Baptists have a different take on that, where it's more congregational and you tend to "follow" what the pastor says, but in reality, the Southern Baptists I knew down in Florida, if they didn't agree with the congregation, they just left.

Explain to me who Roger Williams was.

Roger Williams was living in Massachusetts Bay Colony, among those seeking religious freedom, but it turned out you had to kind of follow the religious culture in Massachusetts. He said it wasn't what he signed up for, so he couldn't get along any more. He articulated this concept of "soul liberty," and he said that ultimately he had to do what God told him to do. He left--took his toys with him, whatever those were--and he went to what's now Rhode Island. That's why Providence has the name Providence. That's the history of Rhode Island. It's a reminder of what can happen. We say we want religious liberty, religious freedom, but the tendency is to always try to force people back into conformity. The relationship of Massachusetts and Rhode Island just reminds us of that. That was my background.

When I got down to Florida State in '83, I just continued the trajectory that I'd already begun. I immediately got involved with Baptist Campus Ministry, Southern Baptist, and fell into the leadership roles. They hired me three different times, not knowing I was gay--I hadn't completely come out yet. One of the things that I do is try to make things work out intellectually and spiritually. I'm just amazed at people who, in junior high, know that they're gay and come out. They know it experientially. I had sex for the first time in the ninth grade and felt tremendous guilt. I didn't have sex for many years after that.

In many ways, my dissertation was about intellectually working out the whole heritage of the Greco-Roman, Judeo-Christian, Western culture. I realized as I was going through this six hundred pages of mental exercise, that in some ways I was coming out to myself and giving myself permission to do that. There were two interesting, quirky things in there.

One, I had a wonderful professor, Karen Laughlin. I could think out loud in the drafts I was giving her. It was a big dissertation, and Karen was wonderful. I put uncertain ideas into content footnotes. I had found this gay adolescent coming-of-age novel in which this gay teen doodling his boyfriend's initials on his notebook, realizes that there were no titles like Mr. or Mrs. that accurately connoted his relationship with his boyfriend. That part of the novel simply illustrated a linguistic theory I was using. What are the constraints of language that permit language to describe only certain things? You could write Mr. and Mrs. and communicate heterosexual relationships clearly, but language conventions permitted no way to communicate other relational realities. I put it into a draft footnote knowing it wouldn't make a final draft but was in the blender--part of what I was thinking. My professor, however, recognized that I was coming out. With no comment, she returned the edited manuscript along with an article that I didn't read at the time, but later realized was one of the founding articles of queer theory. She affirmed my soul liberty to be gay.

Do you think you were in denial and didn't want to recognize being gay?

I think it was scary for me to wonder who I could tell. I couldn't tell people

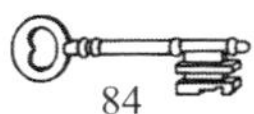

in the religious community but, to an academic liberal, this was fine. She was supportive. Gradually, I started to tell people when I realized what was going on. I started telling other friends of mine, two at a time, because I guessed I could handle two rejections at once. I don't think that's true. I have trouble with one rejection.

The second thing was that I had a wonderful friend, Manuela, from Munich, who was in my program. She once told me about a friend of hers who came out to her as a lesbian, and Manuela said, "This is wonderful. Let's have a celebration." She threw her a party. Those were the kind of friends I was hanging out with in academic circles.

At the same time I was trying to work through gay identity, I was in contact with a friend of mine through a previous life with music. He lived in Ann Arbor, where he went to school. I had him come to Florida and I set up a tour for evangelism--part of my job was evangelistic outreach. So I had my friend Doug come down and do some concerts, and it all went very well. We stayed in touch by mail and I told him I wasn't comfortable being labeled gay. His reply was that you need to pick the label that's the closest fit and then make it your own. As we start to do that, people will recognize that the definitions need to change. So, he got married to his partner at an Episcopalian Church in Ann Arbor. I'm sure Doug took the label and made it look religious and respectable.

I view identity labels as off-the-rack clothing. "Do I want the small, the medium, the large, or the extra large?" You get four choices. Which one is the best fit? When I went though all the available categories, I realized that straight didn't fit. The only label that did fit was gay, and I said, "I guess that's as good as I'm going to get, given the categories." I had started trying it on by coming out to friends down in Tallahassee, and then, by the time I graduated and came up here--I was forty--I had worked through it intellectually, which was important for me in order for it to make sense. It was never any problem spiritually, because I believed way too much that God loved me--the John 3:16--to the consternation of people who want the Bible not to mean that. The very basic knowledge that Jesus loves me is enough.

When I got back to Wichita, I knew I didn't want to do institutional Church. I can do it for about ten years and then need to take time to experience Church as non-institutional. I learn a lot during those times. Right now, I'm overdue.

When you do non-institutional, how does that play out? Do you do a retreat?

I haven't structured it but, I find I can't turn it off. I listen to church-related stuff or read theology, or recognize the religious or spiritual outside of the church building.

When I got back to Wichita, I didn't want to do institutional church, but I found myself sitting in the Lazy Boy watching First United Methodist services on TV every week. I'm singing hymns to the TV and thinking that this was silly. I needed to be in a community. If I was going to be tuned in every Sunday, why not just go somewhere? I went to St. John's Episcopal Church, because I had played the piano at a storefront Episcopalian church, and had been involved with a campus Episcopalian group, so it felt pretty familiar. I went downtown for about nine months, and there was a row of us gay guys. They loved us because we sang well. We sat down in the front so we could have eye contact with the priest, but it felt too sedate. There was only that one lively row. When the priest was reassigned and they sent in somebody else, I just didn't respond to him. Most of the guys in that row went to College Hill United Methodist Church because there was this charismatic pastor there. The first time I went, though, because I'm so deviant and churchy, I found a Sunday school class. That's when I went into Chuck's class. It didn't have a name then. They'd been going six to twelve months before I got there. Once I met Chuck, we clicked. What he didn't say in his interview was that he phoned me the next week to thank me for coming to class and asked me if we could get together sometime so that I could tell my spiritual journey. I'd been hungry for someone to actually care about me. Nobody had really done that. In most churches, people just aren't asked the direct question. So we went out to a Thai restaurant and just talked. I knew this could be a great friendship because he cared about the right things and he didn't feel awkward about asking, "How are you doing spiritually and how can I help you?" He's been very helpful, not only to me, but to that whole class. I've seen him over the last ten years through his different pastorates--decades later people still view him as their pastor. I found myself being United Methodist, but still Baptist. A lot of people are like that. They come from some other tradition, yet they learn something about United Methodism and about Wesley and whatever else is effective for them.

I guess that fits right in with Wesley's comment that you have to work out your own salvation.

A lot of us are doing that. Soon after that, I ended up having to come out to my family. I ended up being a volunteer executive secretary for an AIDS organization. I wrote a grant to the Kansas Department of Health and it won.

The idea was innovative at the time, and it could have gotten some splash. I didn't want to risk that my parents would see "AIDS grant" and my name in the paper, the state's biggest paper. I thought that would be a rudely impersonal and public way to learn your son was gay. If my parents would see this, or someone would have asked them if they'd seen it, that wouldn't be good. So I went over and told only them that I was gay--not being sure how much of it registered. The miscalculation on my part was how my honesty would put them in the closet. I can be amazingly slow on the uptake, and I didn't see that coming. Within twenty-four hours, my mom was distressed and crying over at my sister's. She and Dad came out to my sister, behind closed doors in my sister's bedroom--to her and her husband. So, there were my nephews, being excluded from the adult whispering and crying in the other room. The guys thought somebody was dying. The boys were all sitting there when the adults came out of the bedroom.

My sister said, "Your Uncle Brian is gay." They said, "Is that all?" Because they thought I must be dying--something must be terribly wrong. They were actually okay with it.

Do you think that helped your mother and sister in supporting you?

I think so. What surprised me about Mom was that she mobilized a support network. She told some of her best friends, her pastor, and my physician, who's one of her best friends. She suddenly had all of these books that she was reading. That really surprised me. The cultural assumption is heteronormativity--what's normal is to be heterosexual, which is why the burden of coming out falls onto non-heterosexuals who deviate from the norm. In those dynamics, the person with the abnormal secret is the one who's in the closet. When you come out to someone, you effectively put that person in the closet. Although I had lived with it all of my life, in varying degrees of awareness, she couldn't cope with it for a day. I think one thing that it tells you is how intense a dynamic it is, being in the closet, the secrecy. Mom formed a support system, not in a PFLAG sort of way, but in order to get her through the distress.

It sounds like she was out to a number of people pretty quickly.

She's proud of her gay son? That's not my family. She did what she needed to do to get through.

That was how I started. After I told a few academic friends and it was okay

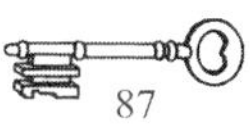

in that sphere of my life, then I told my family. I was going to tell them first. I'm a planner, and PhDs can follow rules for a long time and very obediently, independently. I was going to tell my mom and then my sister, and then branch out until I'd told enough people. Coming out is just a constant, exhausting process. You don't ever really have to come out if you're straight, but you have to if you're not. I was just going to do it until it felt like I was out.

At church, people just make assumptions and I'm okay with that. Let them assume what they want because for the most part that's okay. I told a few people at work and I'm sure a few people just made assumptions. I told my supervisor and a couple of coworkers, because I needed enough verbal declaration and honesty to feel honest.

Chuck interjected an amusing story here. He told about going with Brian to one of the Christmas parties given by Brian's employers. It was at the home of one of the heads of a department. Chuck was sitting next to a woman on a couch, a younger lady who was a coworker of Brian's. They were having a great time visiting. She was a lesbian and she knew he was gay, so they didn't think anything about it. Later, after he had expressed interest in a recipe, one of the employees gave the lady on the couch next to him a recipe for her husband. They all got a chuckle out of it.

B: She just assumed that because they were sitting next to each that they must be married, and that if he had an interest in a recipe, she could just give that recipe to his wife. We always laugh about that. People just make sense of things how they want to.

I came out enough to feel adequate, and I wanted to get involved to change things. That's guided my involvement in Viceroy.

Explain the story behind naming your Sunday school class Viceroy.

There was a sermon illustration from the pastor at College Hill about the Viceroy butterfly. It's a Darwinian explanation about adaptive process. The Viceroy butterfly tastes sweet and is in constant danger of being devoured by hungry predators. The Monarch butterfly is distasteful and predators avoid it. Viceroys learned to pass for the common Monarch in order to appear unappealing, hide their tastiness, and survive. We recognized it as a metaphor--a compelling story that's rich with meaning. People have asked why we're named after a cigarette but it's not that. The metaphor gave the class a name. I'm always nudging Chuck to teach certain things, certain books and chapters. That's the academic side of me. Then he does the hard work of going out in front of the classroom to do the teaching. We did the "Claiming the Promise" study from Reconciling National. We were the first group to do it. We did it off galley proofs from the publisher and it made sense to culminate that with a decision to declare ourselves a Reconciling Sunday school class. We were taking the temperature of the group, which was in total agreement. We did follow-up to give "Claiming the Promise" feedback on the study.

Say more about the study itself. How did it come to be and what was it about?

I don't know the exact history, but there was a writer in the Chicago area named Mary Jo Osterman, who wanted to write a formal, Bible-based curriculum that would not be explicitly anti-gay, which would invite people to look at scriptures and to think about them in a way they hadn't done before. It was structured so that you could do it in several different formats, usually a chapter a week. People found it very easy to read. At that time, in the mid 90's, the culture at College Hill was ready for it. We had quite a good participation. Some people came every week, some came some weeks, but not many came only once and quit. Upon culmination of that study, it made sense for us to give people an opportunity to clarify and codify their beliefs. I synthesized several Reconciling statements from different groups that I found on the Internet. We picked our images and metaphors. We were the first group--not a congregation, not an Annual Conference committee--but the first Sunday school group to declare ourselves Reconciling.

Talk about some of the conference and national level work that you do.

I kept pushing and ended up on national stuff. It kind of jumped from local Viceroy involvement, with congregational support, but the congregation was ambivalent about whether or not it wanted to formalize its label. Academically, this all goes to identity politics. That's the buzzword from the '80s and '90s. The concepts are academically well known, but are often scary to people in the mainstream culture and churches. It's all about whether you should label yourself or claim a certain identity, like Reconciling. It's interesting, because the culture is so diffused and permeated by brand names like Tommy Hilfiger and Polo shirts--just putting the brand name out there where it's visible. But

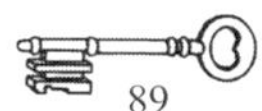

when it comes to other parts of our lives, we're very squeamish about it.

It's interesting to watch the contradictions in dynamic operation. The Judicial Council of the United Methodist Church tried, as Barney Fife would say, to do some 'bud-nipping.' They said to stop identifying yourself as a conservative or liberal, a member of the Good News or Confessing Movements, or Reconciling. You can't label yourself only in certain parts of your lives, and I'm not sure how they can enforce anything as pervasive and complex as identification. Within the United Methodist Church you can label yourself anything you want as an individual. The ruling tried to stop identification at formal, institutional levels of the church in congregations and conferences. I believe there are moments in which honesty, integrity, and justice demand that we label ourselves. They clarify confusion and contradiction, for yourself and for others. When you go shopping and know exactly what you want, it's much easier to find it--and you're quicker to realize this place will never meet your needs.

So College Hill has not become a Reconciling Congregation.

No, there wasn't enough consensus. A few years ago, a marketing consultant convened focus groups, yielding items for a survey that went to the entire congregation of 1700. There was a very high response rate. Ninety-three percent of the congregation said that everyone should be welcome at College Hill, "regardless of sexual orientation." But when it came to labeling that belief clearly for the world to see, one third said "yes," one third said "no," and one third didn't answer. Something happens to many people when you ask them to shift from disclosing a personal belief to committing themselves to a public group with a publicized belief. I am one of those people who will clearly say, "Yes, This is what I believe. Theologically, this is where I must go."

When it comes to your conference and national involvement, is your focus mainly on gay/lesbian issues or justice issues in general?

I would rather focus on justice issues in general, but because of the time when I'm here on earth it feels like the key issue right now is dismantling heterosexism and working on gay rights. I've ended up working on that. I really would like to be working on other things. The stuff I've been doing with Grace Med Clinic really deals with economic justice affecting people's health.

Is that what you do where you work?

The Grace Med Clinic project grew out of a sermon during Lent. The pastor said he was supposed to tell us to give up something like chocolate during Lent. He said, "If you want to give up chocolate for forty days during Lent, do what you have to do but don't make me preach the same old sermon. What I want you to do, if you will, for forty days, is something only you can do." I knew that I could win a grant, so I went privately to two people, a pastor and a clinic director, and volunteered to write a grant to get them some money. The first didn't materialize on the pastor's end, and my arrival at the clinic was bad timing. I didn't let go of the idea, however. The clinic idea kept nagging me. I went back a year later. There had been a change in clinic personnel, and the new director asked me to sit down. It was a whole different atmosphere. I introduced myself and told her I had come to ask what she needed. She rattled off six things, and I selected two. One was to launch their women's cancer screening program--the other was new carpeting, which I decided to do on the side.

That was at St. Paul's United Methodist Church, twenty years ago. Some Latina women had asked for affordable healthcare, so Chuck started a clinic in the church's education building during the week as a normal response to neighborhood need. I asked him if he knew anybody with money or ties to somebody connected to a carpet store. He did, and I asked him if it would be hard to visit with that person and get some carpet. He thought he could, and he came back the following Sunday with carpet. Another friend arranged for the installation. I wrote the grant that funded the women's cancer program, which is still going well. Some sermons matter.

Some people at the Conference associate my presence--my face, my name, anything I'm going to say or write--only with gays or only with sex or with being radical--whatever scary word comes to mind. This is today's justice issue, and I'm not going to duck it. It just happens that I would benefit from the love and acceptance. I would benefit from some of that directly, so some people say that invalidates my motives. The perfect advocate--some straight person with no "gay motive," whose nephew's not gay, for example--could actually have more clout. We need those people to say that because of grace reasons, theological reasons, and justice reasons, "Here I stand."

Is this a frustrating time for you politically? Do you feel like we're going backwards?

No, really, I don't. It makes me sad, you know, the fact that the legislature

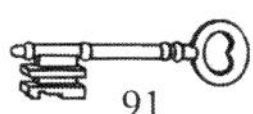

voted this week--although narrowly--to send the anti-gay marriage amendment to the voters in April. It's very sad, and it feels personal. It feels like a collective injustice. It's going to be shot down for Constitutional reasons by the Judiciary. Because they're thinking in terms of principles and case law in doing their jobs, those judges are going to be improperly maligned as "activist" judges. It seems to me that the only people who pejoratively use the term "activists" are those who want inaction. What we've got is an inactive response to peoples' democratic needs and rights. It's frustrating. I just think those critics are there and ultimately, America is going to do the right thing.

People have said that I need to move to a different place but, in therapeutic terms that would be the so-called geographic solution. Right now the solution isn't to move to California, New York, or New Jersey. I am here, and this is where I need to do something, so that's what I do.

Are you guided or inspired by any particular scripture?

Those "therefore" passages in Romans--like in 3, 6, 8, and 12--are very strong. My approach is an old Navigator's idea. I try to be guided by the "whole counsel of Scripture," not by particular verses. I was reared to be able to pull isolated verses out and, hopefully, to be able to use them correctly. However, it's so easy to proof text, especially in Proverbs. I think you can prove anything in Proverbs because it's not a systematic argument, as in Romans, which I find useful to read backwards. Paul wanted to end with a certain conclusion, and it's very logically outlined. That's why it really bugs me to see people quote Romans 1:26-28 out of context. An anti-gay person came up to me once and wanted to read Romans 1 to me, and I said to him, "Let's read the first three chapters. I love Romans!"

Well, he didn't want to get to Romans 2 because early in chapter 2, Paul completely upends everything he said at the end of chapter 1, because he was trying to say, "Everybody's in one category--everybody's in one boat--all are sinners. Jesus loves us all--God loves us all--seek after God." It frustrated this person when I wanted to read more Scripture. I didn't want to let him stop too soon. I knew what was coming in the story. So, I don't like to look at isolated verses, although those are very helpful sometimes, but I try to look at the whole counsel.

I mentioned earlier liking John 3:16, the idea of "whosoever," and then going on into 3:17, that God didn't send Jesus into the world to condemn the world. That verse sends you off into the abundant life and all those ideas. We can find our wholeness in God--the images of the branch and the vineyard and all that. I try to retain those stories and those ideas. As I get older, I find that I'm guided by the whole counsel and not solely by the verses I memorized in the fourth grade.

[Here Chuck injects a comment suggesting Brian talk about the three years of leadership he had spent on the National Reconciling Board.]

B: You can't always tell if you're doing any good. You hope you have some influence. It's been encouraging seeing all sorts and types of people getting involved in the national scene while trying to balance their local efforts. Once I'm done with my national obligation, I know I'm going to get involved with stuff differently, locally. I haven't figured out how yet.

Do you have any thoughts about the Open Hearts, Open Minds, Open Doors motto as a goal set forth by the Church?

You know, in some ways I think we already have it, but some people are fighting it so adamantly because they are trying to close doors and close minds. I think they're ineffective at "hearts". I think hearts are already open, but some people, for whatever motive, for whatever reason, so fear it or so hate it, that they are actively trying to close what is already open. They are trying to create division where there is unity. I see it as a matter of their wearing out. They are going to be unable to close what God wants open-- what already is open!

There has been disagreement on the board for National Reconciling about how we felt about the denomination using that phrase. The "Open the Doors" campaign was one of Reconciling Network's activities at the Denver General Conference. From one perspective, it looked like the denomination had co-opted the phrase, added two more, and turned it into a big marketing campaign, but they hadn't changed their substance. That's how some people interpreted it. As I see it, there is openness on these three key fronts--it is real and it is happening. People won't be able to stop it. I don't think it's going to stop. I think it is going to be a matter of the people who insist on closing and dividing and denying grace and love getting weary. Then they'll need healing and acceptance, and they'll need comfort. They're going to feel bad when this is all better resolved. My hope is that they won't feel shame, and that people who are now Reconciling won't lord it over them, but will say, "Oh, come on in."

Is that a good note on which to end?

Bishop Richard B. Wilke

Room at the Foot of the Cross

I had heard Bishop Wilke's name in connection with the Disciple Bible Study Series for years and had great respect for his work in that area. Having taken all of the Disciple courses available through my local church, I was aware that Bishop Wilke knew his Bible. I appreciated the way the series was written, encouraging the sharing of ideas and experiences, not with cut-and-dried answers from one person's viewpoint. His wife, Julia, was involved in its development, as well.

Although the bishop and his wife had served a local congregation in my hometown of Salina, I had not met him at that time, but I had read an article he had written later for a booklet put together by the Northaven United Methodist Church in Dallas, Texas, entitled Finishing the Journey: Questions and Answers from United Methodists of Conviction. *All of the articles in the booklet had something to do with homosexuality and the Church.*

Even though my book of interviews was to focus on personal faith stories, I knew that in some way the troublesome scriptures on homosexuality had to be included, so when a friend of mine suggested interviewing Bishop Wilke. I thought it was a great idea.

On the day the interview was scheduled, Julia met me with warm hospitality at the front door of their home. We sat and visited for a few minutes while we waited for Bishop Wilke to join us. She told me she was preparing the house and yard for an upcoming 80th birthday party for her husband. Bishop Wilke entered the room with a stack of books, including the Bible, tucked under his arm. I hoped that meant my goal of dealing with those troublesome scriptures was going to be met. Not only was that goal met, but I spent a delightful afternoon with the Bishop, getting to know his warm personality and his interesting story of faith.

Could you share with me some of your background in the Church? Where did you grow up, and what was your early religious life like?

Bishop Wilke: I grew up in El Dorado, Kansas, and my dad was a funeral director. He had the emergency ambulance, and of course I was helping, as early as I was able to lift one end of the cot or whatever. The great thing about that was that I saw all aspects of life. As a teen-ager going to the hospital, going out on wrecks at three in the morning, I saw people who had died of all different causes. My dad was a very non-judgmental person, and he was also very fair to everybody--black or white. Every black family in town called Dad when they had a death because they got a first-class funeral. Everybody was the same.

That's wonderful.

Then I went to SMU and met Julia there. She was from Texarkana. Then I went to Yale for seminary, and we got married. My first church was in Scandia, Kansas, a country church. My next church was a mission church in Wichita, a new church, seven years old, Pleasant Valley. Then I went to University Church, Salina, Kansas. That was fun--a lot of college students and professors--more of a preaching church. Later I was on the District here in Winfield for about three years, followed by First Church, Wichita for eleven years. After that they elected me bishop, and I was in Arkansas for twelve years.

Did you retire from there?

Well, they call me Bishop in Residence at Southwestern College which means I help a little around the edges.

Did you go to church as a child?

Yes, I was raised in the Methodist church in El Dorado. Mom and Dad were laity. Mom taught Sunday school, Dad was usually on the finance committee or trustee committee. I went to Sunday school and church every Sunday, youth fellowship, youth camps--I was very involved. It was an active time for youth in the Methodist Church. There was a very strong youth program all over the country.

In Kansas that means going to Camp Horizon.

Yes, I did Camp Horizon, Camp Wood with the Y, Camp Wentz, down in

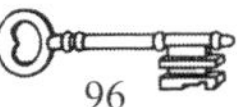

Ponca City, in Boy Scouts, Philmont Scout Ranch. I did a lot of that.

You said that your dad was very non-judgmental. Did you get that same attitude from your church during your growing-up years?

Yes, my church was quite open. I'd say it tended to be on the liberal side. It was after World War II when I was a high school student, and the sermons were "We're going to feed a hungry world"-- "We're going to have peace now, all over the world forever"-- "We're going to have racial justice". We didn't have much integration, but at least we were taught that. We were still Christ-centered and Wesleyan, but we were a bit idealistic in the world view that I was taught.

Would you say that they paid attention to the prophets?

Yes, I think so. A little bit more just to the words of Christ, being peacemakers, and "I was hungry"--Matthew 25.

When did you actually feel your call to the ministry?

That was when I was seventeen. We went to a huge youth conference in Cleveland, Ohio, with over ten thousand youth. The great preachers of the day were a man named Richard Raines, who later became a bishop, and E. Stanley Jones. They lifted up the call of Christ for your life, not only to the ministry but "Christ is calling you to give your heart." I felt called to preach, and from then on I was convinced of that.

Did you have a chance to do that in your local church?

Oh, yes, the pastors would have me give devotions, or three of us would give the sermon when I was a senior in high school. Some country churches, Rosalia and Towanda, would have me come and preach when I was a senior in high school, and then again when I was home during my freshman year in college.

Did you have anyone you called a mentor?

I never really had a mentor. I wish I had. I had pastors who would ask me how I was doing, but I never really had a mentor. I worked as an associate for two years while I was in seminary, but didn't really get a lot of supervision.

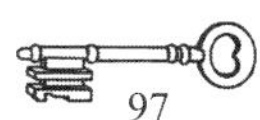

I guess you might say you kind of worked out your own salvation.

Yeah, I guess I worked out my own salvation with counsel from some along the way.

You and your wife, Julia, have been instrumental in starting the Disciple Bible Study and writing it. How did that come about?

This has been a big, big thing. In Wichita we began to realize that people didn't know the Scriptures. We tried to start new adult Sunday school classes, and we couldn't get teachers, because they didn't know what they needed to teach. What we were sensing then is now quite prevalent. People like George Gallop say that six out of ten college students can't name the four Gospel writers, and eighty percent can't name three of the Ten Commandments. We've had forty years of no Bible teachings in the schools, and Sunday Schools are in decline, and so forth. Well, we began to sense that, and we also did a marriage therapy group. The doctors and lawyers in Salina, when they found out I was interested in counseling, started sending people to me. We put a group together for a year, and then we put another group together for a year, so we learned a little bit about small group life. That perceived lack of knowledge from our laity, especially people under forty at that time and fifty today--they didn't know the Scriptures, and we were getting the sense of the hunger people have for some kind of fellowship.

I have to say that I've taken all four of the Disciple studies and the follow-up studies and have thoroughly enjoyed them.

Well, it gets you into the Scriptures, and not in a literalist, fundamentalist way.

That's what I have appreciated about it--the way it was written. Were you intentional about the writing, making sure it was a broad-based study?

We were intentional that people should encounter the text without theological spin--in other words, not putting a Methodist or Baptist spin to it or saying, "This is what it means." We wanted to let people read it, and in the freedom of the group let people say, "Oh I don't agree with that," or "What do you think," or "I have a different experience with that". We just wanted to let the conversation take place, which we think is a Wesleyan way. In fact, one of our leaders, one of our guides, a man by the name of Dr. Albert Outler of Perkins School of Theology at SMU, said that what we're hoping for is the Wesley class meeting. These were the class meetings that Wesley put in homes where people would talk and study and pray and hold each other accountable.

I think that is what's happened. In every class I've been in it's been different--different combinations of people. At Trinity, people come from all kinds of backgrounds--United Methodist, Catholic, Baptist--so we get all those takes on Scripture. Even each of the presenters on the videos that are part of the format is different in style and background.

We have a wide diversity on those tapes, a Jewish rabbi, a Roman Catholic priest and others. We also have thirty different denominations that are using this, so that's nice.

Did you have any idea when you were putting that series together that you would end up looking more closely at the verses having to do with homosexuality?

We began writing in 1986 when the homosexual issue was just beginning. Only one time did an editor ask me if I was going to deal with homosexuality. I told him, "no," that I was just going to let people read the text. Actually, the Scriptures have very little to say about homosexuality. The scholars, both conservative and liberal--a conservative scholar like Richard Hayes of Duke, a liberal scholar like John Holbert of Perkins--if they were sitting here, would say the word "homosexual" or "homosexuality" is never used in the Scriptures in Hebrew or Greek. It's not mentioned at all, so that's one thing. Some of the passages referred to by the angry, vitriolic homophobics are misread by them. They use them out of context and misunderstand them. So, no, we did the whole Disciple study without ever lifting up the issue, partly because we were just trying to flow with the text.

I know you have done some writing since that, an article for the publication Finishing the Journey.

Finishing the Journey was done by the North Haven United Methodist Church in Dallas. Different ones of us wrote short articles for it. John Holbert, professor at Perkins, wrote an article for it, and I told him I wouldn't write my article unless he wrote his, because he's a true Bible scholar. John Thornburg's a pastor, Joe Allen is a professor of ethics, Dr. McElvaney was the president of

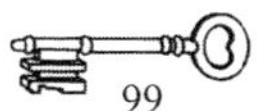

St. Paul's Seminary and Robin Lovin was dean of Perkins. They all had articles in the booklet.

I notice you have Peter Gomes' book *The Good Book* among your references. I have that book in my library and consider it to be an excellent resource.

Okay, if you have it, then you know that he is at Harvard, is Black and gay. A fellow bishop recommended it to me. His chapter on homosexuality, I thought, was brilliant. One of the things I like is that he talks about how some people want to put rape and prostitution together with homosexuality with all the single bars in big cities. All they knew of homosexuality was prostitution and pedophilia, lasciviousness, which I would call fornication and exploitation. Really, in the Bible, those are usually dealing with heterosexuals. But, anyway, the point is, as a scholar and a gay man, Gome's work is terrific.

Did you base your article on the information found in his work?

You realize that scholars claim the words "homosexual" and "homosexuality" aren't even in the Bible. That's important. Then, I've been asked what the Bible says about marriage. Once I was kind of trying to be a little cute, but still they asked. I said, "Well, you have the father of Israel and the father of our faith, Abraham, who had one wife and one concubine. Then there's Jacob, the father of the twelve tribes of Israel, who had two wives and two concubines." I said, "Then, of course, there's King David. They list seventeen wives by name, and the next verse says he had many other wives and concubines too numerous to mention. We're talking about the Bible, now. We're talking about marriage in the Bible. Then there's King Solomon. He had seven hundred wives and three hundred concubines." By this time, they're usually starting to giggle a little. Well, you asked about Bible marriages. Then I said, "You have Saint Paul who didn't marry and advised people not to marry if they could avoid it so they could give their lives fully to the gospel." Then you have Jesus. They asked him about eunuchs, a word thought to describe people who weren't interested in marriage. He said some were born eunuchs and some chose to be eunuchs. That's been a little bit of the basis of the Catholic priesthood.

Then they want to ask about Sodom. Well, I said, "The prophet Ezekiel was very clear--the sins of Sodom were two things. One was this vile inhospitality, and second, he said they had pride, excess of food, prosperous ease, and did not aid the poor and the needy.

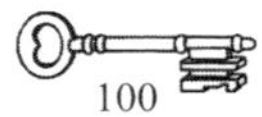

They were not a Godly people. That's the prophet Ezekiel telling the sins of Sodom. Jesus refers to Sodom almost always, and in one place particularly, as the sin of inhospitality. When strangers came the town's people wanted to violently attack, so that's biblical, but is often misinterpreted.

As I consider the biblical material, I just can't escape from my theology that Jesus is Lord! That's my theology. Someone once said, "The Bible is my authority." the Bible has never claimed to be our absolute authority. The Bible is not God. The Bible points us to God. The Bible is there for guidance to introduce us to God--to introduce us to Christ, but the Bible says that no one can say Jesus is Lord except by the Holy Spirit. So, that is to me my bedrock. You asked about my early life. When I was fourteen, a guy from Wichita came over and spoke to our youth group. He said, "There are a lot of stars and planets moving around, but there's one North Star. Jesus is the North Star. If you give your life to him he will not play false with you." I came up and knelt and gave my life to Jesus.

Well. The point is--what did Jesus do? Restrictive laws? Restrictive covenant? No. He was reaching out to bring people in. As you know, he reached out to tax collectors, so-called sinners, who were really people who were ceremonially unclean. I grew up in a funeral home. If you touch a dead body, according to the Torah, you're ceremonially unclean and you'd need to have a washing purification rite before you can worship. If you even take a dead animal out of the ditch on the farm or a lot of things, it makes you ceremonially unclean. Jesus ate dinner with these people. Of course, we have the woman at the well, married five times. I've often thought about why she was married five times. You know what I think? I think she couldn't bear children. One thing people forget is why people married and how people married in biblical times. They married at age thirteen, fourteen, fifteen, usually family arranged. Why did they marry? They married to have children to carry on the family inheritance. It was an economic thing, not a sexual thing, but an economic thing. The young man and this young woman are not old enough to know what they're doing. The arrangement is made. Martin Luther says that Mary, the mother of Jesus, couldn't have been older than fifteen or sixteen. Anyway, those marriages were arranged for economic reasons. You've got your little family farm and that's all you have, and you have no way of survival except holding onto that family inheritance. So, that marriage union was very important. Well, anyway, I think if she couldn't bear children, she was considered worthless as a wife. It makes sense to me. But, she was very important in Jesus' ministry.

This brings up a point that is very important to me in my faith journey, and in relating to the homosexual community. God and Jesus both used people in society who were considered outcasts to do their work. I wonder if we are missing the boat by not taking a look at what God might be trying to teach us through the gay community. Do you have any thoughts about that concept?

One of the things I sometimes say is, "Is there room for love in the Church?". Some people want to be so judgmental. Jesus was strong on this point. Judge not, lest ye be judged. With the judgment you give out, you'll be judged. Wow! Judge not! I've been studying the word "love" in the Bible. Everyone--John, I John, Paul's thirteenth chapter of Corinthians, Peter--over and over, because of the diversity of the early Church, they just kept saying, "You've got to love each other." Jesus' ministry was constantly reaching out to those who were excluded from the community.

These days we say exclusion is the result of fear. Do you think that was the case then, too?

I guess so. You know, I was just amazed at this marriage amendment. People would say it's a threat to marriage. In fact last Sunday I was preaching in Fayetteville, Arkansas, and I said that in Kansas we'd passed this. I was told it would threaten my marriage. That's not a threat to my marriage. Adultery is the biggest threat to a marriage--not two guys living together. That's not a threat to my marriage.

Have you always been as open about homosexuality as you are now?

I would like to talk about the fact that I have come a long way in my own understanding. We didn't used to have homosexuals. On our farms we had one of the boys who didn't marry, and we called them "single men," and they stayed home with Mom and Dad on the farm. Some of them were very lonely, some of them went to church, and some of them didn't. Then we had school teachers. In El Dorado, Kansas, if you were a single school teacher, you weren't allowed to marry. If you married, you were fired. If you were already married and they hired you, that was one thing--but if you were single, you stayed single. My grandmother had schoolteachers live upstairs in her big old house for forty years. She made a little money, and she was a widow. They lived together. They taught Sunday school, taught the third graders.

We didn't have homosexuals. People would say things like, "Beverly, where's your son? He's such a gifted musician. He's gone to New York and he's in a band." Or they'd say, "Terry, where's your son?" And they'd talk about his being an artist and studying art in San Francisco. We didn't have homosexuals. It wasn't even discussed.

One guy in my high school we thought was a little effeminate, the way he acted, but the word "homosexual" just wasn't in our thinking. Another example: When I was pastor of a church, a fellow in my youth fellowship was the most popular, best looking, brightest guy, valedictorian of the class, but he just didn't date--it never occurred to me. Years later he died of AIDS, married with two children. At another church, there was a talented guy in the congregation. The summer after he graduated from high school, his dad called me and said his son wanted to go to Yale. Since I had been to Yale, could I write him a letter? We got him in there. I didn't think about his being homosexual or anything. He sang in the choir at Yale and about his junior year, he died of AIDS. Well, now we're beginning to get some visibility.

I helped write the United Methodist Church's rule in '84 called "faithfulness in marriage, celibacy in single-hood." I voted for it. I didn't know anything about homosexuality. Well, gradually, as I've talked to people as they've come out in the open, it's made a difference, you see. I was preaching at a church the other day, and I said something about homosexuality. Two women who had sung in the choir for thirty years invited us to lunch and nothing was actually said. One was a business woman, and the other was a professional woman. I noticed one of the women had a ring on her second finger just like I do, but nothing was ever said. When I think of the churches I've been in where the organist went to lunch with the tenor I begin to look at things differently. Another example with women--the Wesleyan Service Guild for professional women was a fellowship of women who never married. Some of those women were communion stewards, taught Sunday school, lived together until they were ninety and then made funeral arrangements for their partners, but nothing was ever said. It wasn't even on the radar screen. But slowly, as people in families began to come out, it made a difference. Julia has a couple of cousins--one's a distinguished attorney with a partner.

I'll tell you a quick story about a pastor in the South who's very conservative and the pastor of a big church. He said to me, "Dick, you won't believe what happened. I have a doctor in the church who was in his seventies, who died

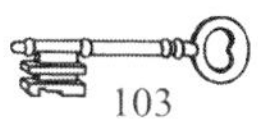

and left the church two and a half million dollars. He said he did it because the church had been his life, and his partner, who is a banker, has all the money he needs." So this pastor realized for the first time that two men who all their lives lived in the same house, and both had honorable, distinguished professions, and everybody in town knew them and dealt with them, but they hadn't ever put that twist to it. So now, this pastor, who is sort of against homosexuality, is having his eyes opened.

Bishop Wilke, what are your thoughts on the future of the Church where homosexuality is concerned?

Okay, Beverly, here are my thoughts on the future. People say this is going to divide the Church. At the big level, the General Conference level, people are going to argue philosophically: "What do you think? What do you think? What about this rule?" At the local level, they deal with people by their name and face: "This is Mary--Oh, she's the third grade teacher. She taught my children. This is Susan--Oh, Susan, she sings in the choir with Mary. They are communion stewards. We've known them all our lives."

I went to a church in Arkansas, a little bitty church. They were having an anniversary, one hundred years or something like that. We went out there, and there were probably fifty people there. They didn't have an organ, just a piano. Here was a young man with a ring in his ear, and my wife turned to me and said, "He's gay." Afterwards, she went to talk to him, but I went to talk to the church leaders. I met the president of the United Methodist Women, the UMW. She was a wonderful leader in the church, had been there forever. Well, this was her son who came out from Little Rock to play for that service. Everybody loved him and hugged him and was thrilled that he was willing to come back to play. They knew him growing up from the day he was born. This was John.

In many local churches, there might be two women who take communion and hold hands, two men in the choir. People know them and love them, and that's what makes the difference.

Now this is my big argument from Scripture. When they had conflict in the early Church over food laws, Sabbath laws, Jews, Gentiles the issue was always: "Have they received the Holy Spirit?" That was the point. That's where conservatives like James, the brother of Jesus, and Barnabus and Paul stuck together. If they love Christ and have received the Holy Spirit (meaning they show love, faith, kindness, long suffering) then they're in. What we have to do in the Church is to oppose rape, pedophilia, promiscuous fornication, incest, any kind of authoritative misuse of children, violence of any kind by anyone of any orientation.

As Peter Gomes says, that's not the same as two women who give their lives to each other in faithfulness.

One thing about the Scriptures, St. Paul has the passage in Romans which is repeated elsewhere, about men having sexual relations with men, women with women. The scholars say that Paul knew two kinds of sexual experience in the Jewish community. One was the Greek patriarchs who bought slave boys. They were pedophiles. Secondly, the heterosexuals worshiped in the temple. They were married, but they worshiped in the temple where there were prostitutes. There was a temple in Corinth, the temple of one thousand prostitutes, the Temple to Athena. There were both men and women prostitutes. That was a form of worship. You had sexual experience, and it was a form of worship to pagan gods. Paul said, "That is an abomination." These were heterosexual people. These were married people. They thought they were worshiping in that form. That is what Paul is referring to in that kind of experience.

Getting back to the issue of the broader Church, do you think the broader denominational Church will ever come to grips with the issue of homosexuality?

Sure, now that the issue has come out of the closet, we'll talk about it for the next thirty years, argue, and be vitriolic. Some will leave the Church for one reason or another. You heard about this big Episcopal Church in Kansas City that left the denomination. Maybe you read about that. My sister's an Episcopalian in a nearby church, and they're shaking their heads at those people. They left the denomination because they have a gay bishop.

I don't know any more about the future than anybody else, but I think at the local level people will realize that their cousin, their son, a lady in the choir, the organist, that these homosexual people are people they know and love. They will love them and they will slowly, at the grass roots level, not at the general level, change. The general Church isn't going to change for quite awhile. With the present mood in our country, if you have a vote, it will be seven to three against. But, I think slowly, just exactly like race relations, it will change. People in the South who had black cooks and housekeepers could be quite prejudiced in general, but their hired help was like family, and if one of them died, they might be the only white people at the funeral. That wasn't a matter of race--it was someone with a name and a face they loved.

Regarding women--look how long it's taken us to have women in normal participation in society's leadership. It didn't start at the top. It started at the bottom.

And so it is with this issue. It starts with families talking about their kids and being "out." We'll start putting different criteria on the thing. Seeing homosexuals in places of importance in the Church and society will change things. Things like this book will change things, but I don't think the Church is going to change for thirty years.

Do you have any comments you want to make, any words of hope for those who want to be accepted in churches and have a supportive place to take their faith journeys?

I go to a lot of different churches, and I can sense whether there is a spirit of love, a spirit of fellowship, a spirit of openness, a spirit of acceptance. I don't like hard, narrow, judgmental churches that are full of hate. I'm not drawn to that. There are several churches that are Reconciling churches and you can feel the love and acceptance. It's marvelous. There's a church in Houston that I've gone to that I like. You mentioned Disciple. There was one young man there who told me that he shared in his Disciple class that he was gay. He was totally accepted and loved there. It put a face on the issue for his class. I just feel like the Gospel of our Lord is a Gospel of love, not hatred.

With Bishop Wilke's permission, I am reprinting his article, "What does the Bible call us, as Christians, to do on this issue?"

I am amazed at my lifelong ignorance of homosexuality. I have spent my ministry dealing mostly with the uses, misuses, and abuses of sex among heterosexuals. But I did not understand (or worry about) my energetic, popular youth fellowship leaders who did not date. I was grateful for the Wesleyan Service Guild women, some of whom lived together and cared for each other for 50 or 60 years. My grandmother housed schoolteachers who ate at the same table, slept in the same room and prayed together in church. I, like most of society, was caught off guard when some of my young friends, committed to the Lord, active in the church, began dying of AIDS.

So I began to explore Scripture and to talk with homosexuals and their families. I discovered that Sodom was destroyed for its violent inhospitality to strangers. The angry, lustful townspeople were eager to rape, violate, maim, and

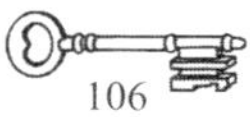

kill the strangers--be they men or women--who were visiting Lot. The prophet Ezekiel wrote (16:49), "This was the guilt of your sister Sodom: She and her daughters had pride, excess of food, and prosperous ease, but did not aid the poor and needy." Jesus implied that Sodom was guilty of ugly inhospitality in Luke 10:10-12.

The Holiness Code in Leviticus and Deuteronomy was designed to set the Jews apart from the Canaanites. It was not a universal morality. It was particular to the Hebrews-and to the times. It reflected one side of the constant tension in Judaism, as well as in all religions, between exclusion and inclusion. For example, no one maimed or castrated could enter the temple (Deuteronomy 23:1), yet Isaiah argued the opposite--that a castrated man who kept the Sabbath was welcome (Isaiah 56:4-5). I've been fascinated with the fact that the first person converted by Philip the Evangelist was a black man, an African eunuch, forbidden by the Holiness Code to go near the temple (Acts 8:26-40). Also, the Holiness Code prohibited marriage to a Gentile (Ezra, for example, made the Jewish men divorce their non-Jewish wives), yet Ruth the Moabite was honored as King David's great-grandmother.

Neither Jews nor Christians obey the Holiness Code today. Christians eat shrimp because Jesus said, "It is not what goes into the mouth that defiles a person, but it is what comes out of the mouth that defiles." (Matthew 15:11). We do not stone those taken in adultery because Jesus said, "Let anyone among you who is without sin be the first to throw a stone at her" (John 8:7). No one today would justify killing children who spoke back to their mother or father (Deuteronomy 21:18).

The prophet Isaiah rebelled at the exclusiveness of the Holiness Code, arguing that people should come from all nations--from the north, south, east and west. "I will give you as a light to the nations that my salvation may reach to the end of the earth." (Isaiah 49:6)

Paul does graphically list sins where women have sex with women, and men with men, but Paul was familiar with only two kinds of homosexual activity: when wealthy Greeks would buy young boys as slaves and play with them sexually, and when part of the Greek-Roman world would go to male and female prostitute/priests as a form of fertility or mystery cult worship. In Romans Chapter 1, Paul was trying to make a point by listing every sin he could think of. He wanted to show that we have all fallen short, that we are all sinners in need of the atoning grace of God. As I reflect on the list of sins, I know not a day goes by but what I am guilty and in need of grace.

But Jesus and his ministry concern me most. He was nearly killed in his

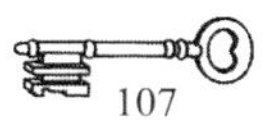

hometown for mentioning that Elisha healed the Assyrian general, Naama, of leprosy. He was continually condemned for touching the leper, for opening the eyes of the blind beggars (who were considered ceremonially unclean), and for talking with a Samaritan woman.

My most soul-shaking scripture is Luke 15:1-2. Jesus drew tax collectors and sinners to himself. Religious leaders grumbled and said, "This fellow welcomes sinners and eats with them." When queried, he told stories about a lost sheep, a lost coin, and a lost boy. His point was this: They were to be brought back into circulation, into community. The context is the inclusive ministry of Jesus for which he was crucified.

As I've said, I've spent a lot of time dealing with people with various sexual issues. I believe sex, like fire, can do a lot of harm and a lot of good. There are many sexual sins-heterosexual and homosexual--that are foreign to faith. Surely our consciences condemn prostitution, pedophilia, rape, promiscuity, and exploitation. But I also believe from scientific data and from conversations with gay men and lesbians and their families, that Christ Jesus can capture the hearts of homosexuals and can lead them into faithful, stable, loving relationships.

When I see two men or two women kneeling together to take Holy Communion, working diligently for human betterment, and caring for each other across the years, I must pause and believe there is room for them in the household of God. As Fanny Crosby says in her hymn, "There is room at the foot of the cross."

Joe and Eric

Gay, Christian, and, Married

When Cleaning Closets was published, our son, Eric, was just out of college with a degree in musical theater. He was living the life of a starving actor in New York City. That was 1995. Cleaning Closets *was the story of my spiritual journey after discovering that I had a son who was gay. Twelve years of family history have occurred since then and Eric is now living in Florida with his life partner, Joe, who is an ordained Metropolitan Community Church pastor. We have never regretted choosing the path of love and acceptance of those we know and care about who are homosexual in their orientation. Our life and faith have been greatly enriched by the people who have been brought to us, one of whom is Joe. We proudly refer to him as our son-in-law. During a weekend visit to attend Rev. Joe's installation into his Florida MCC congregation, this interview was done.*

It had been a weekend of activity including reunions with two of Joe's sisters and Penny, the senior pastor of the San Francisco Metropolitan Church where Eric and Joe met. I had met many of the congregants of the Trinity Metropolitan Church that Joe was now serving and a group of friends Joe and Eric got together with once a week for fun and relaxation. The installation had been inspiring and, as was typical of their household, followed by hospitality, food, laughter and celebration offered to everyone.

After the guests had gone and the food was put away I sat down with Joe and Eric in their living room to do this interview.

Eric, talk about your early years in the church.

Eric: I grew up in the United Methodist Church, which was a big part of my development and a big part of our family life. I don't recall it being a judgmental environment as far as the gay issue goes. I do remember when I realized I was

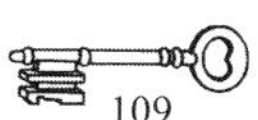

gay and felt conflicted about being Christian and gay. The more people I've met since we've been working in the church and hearing people's stories about growing up gay and Christian, I've concluded that I wasn't in an oppressive environment, as far as that goes. Somehow I got the message that I couldn't be gay and Christian, but I don't remember hearing that preached from the pulpit. I feel like it was a fairly healthy environment to grow up in. It sort of taught me how to be in the world, how to treat people--that sort of thing.

Joe: I grew up in the Catholic Church and the youngest of six children. A lot of what I learned wasn't necessarily taught to me, but it was understood just because of the actions and practices of other people around me. I had grandparents, parents and siblings all ahead of me to set examples. Rarely did I have to ask questions because everything was right there in front of me. We were only two blocks from the church and school, so our lives did center a lot on the church and church community. Our neighborhood was actually a neighborhood that was conceived by the parish priest for Catholics with large families. With six children, we were one of the smaller families. It permeated our culture. Being Catholic was the whole thing. That was the most important part of growing up.

Was homosexuality ever mentioned in the context of this culture?

J: Not at all. Not a word. Neither was it mentioned in the Lebanese community which was another part of my culture. There was a relative of a relative of mine that everyone distanced themselves from. There was a sort of "Oh! What a shame" expression on people's faces or in their tone when he was mentioned. This guy, at that time in his forties, lived with his mother. There was just something creepy about him. I don't even know if it was him as much as it was how he was marginalized in a way, not by word or action, but just by understanding. It was the same way our faith was understood without it being spelled out. There was this feeling that he was off to the side somewhere. At that time it seemed appropriate, which is really strange, but that's how I grew up feeling about him, because that's how everyone treated him. He was in the community, but not in the community.

Eric, the focus of one of the chapters in *Cleaning Closets* highlighted your struggle with thinking you couldn't be gay and Christian. How did you finally reconcile that question?

E: When *Cleaning Closets* came out I was just out of college, and as many

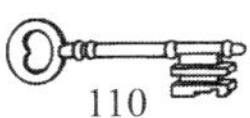

students that age, I had gone through college distancing myself from church. The turning point for me was probably after college when I was working in Oregon doing a Christmas show. I was in Ashland, a small town where there is a really interesting spiritual community. One of the women working in the show, Rebecca, was a very spiritual person. Her spirituality was based more on nature, focusing on the seasons, the sun and moon. Holidays or rituals were based more on the solstices, the natural calendar. The cast in this particular show was made up of people of different spiritualities, and I specifically learned from her that I could make rituals that meant something to me. She didn't follow any doctrine necessarily, any particular rules. I had never considered that I didn't need a special conduit or rule book in order to have a relationship with God. That's when I started getting back to spirituality--on my terms--what made sense to me. She taught me about creating rituals and infusing them with whatever meant something to me. In the Christian church, for me specifically the United Methodist Church, the rituals that were connected to particular events in the liturgical year sometimes began to lose meaning. I just did them because I was supposed to. I found that it was a whole new way of communicating with God when I was creating the ritual to symbolize what I needed to focus on. That might be lighting a candle and praying through it as a conduit to God. It was then that my spiritual journey began to mean something to me again. I explored different religions, different cultures, and did a lot of reading. When people asked me about my religion during that time of exploration, I told them I was kind of free-lancing. I was curious about other religions and cultures and took what made sense to me and made it my own. I found it very freeing. When I was in Los Angeles, I went to a church that mixed eastern and western religions, focusing on Christ and some gurus from the eastern traditions. They focused a lot on meditation as a spiritual practice to get to God. Eventually, I moved to San Francisco and found MCC, Metropolitan Community Church. By then, my relationship with God felt right and made sense. I had my ways of communicating that. After that, that community--the people at that church--then became another conduit to God. It all kind of became a ministry, connecting with those people. In a way it was coming full circle, because community was a big part of growing up in the United Methodist Church. Those people were important in my younger development, as these people were in my adult life.

Joe, did you experience a break from the church during your college years, as well?

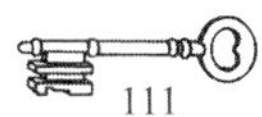

J: I was actually in seminary my freshman year in college, the Christian Brothers. I had that influence in my family with a brother who had been in the seminary for five years. There was an expectation out of Catholic families, again unspoken, that one or more of the children would go into religious life. There was a whole different understanding, to my knowing, of what a calling meant. Or perhaps it just hadn't been explained to me what that was. Part of my early years, my early development, taught me I was different, but I didn't know how. By the time I knew it had to do with sexuality I just knew that being different wasn't a good thing. That was a direct conflict with the faith tradition. Again, it wasn't spelled out anywhere, I just knew. The norm was that you were either in religious life or you were in a heterosexual relationship. Also, there was a conflict, because growing up in the Catholic faith, especially in those days, it was taught that it was the one true faith, there was no other option, the Catholic way or no way. I guess you would say the Jewish faith was the next best thing, but for me, they didn't have it quite right because they didn't recognize Jesus Christ. Again, this was unspoken, but it permeated everything. You didn't question. Faith was blind, and not in a good sense. If you were in pain, you offered it up. You didn't try to fix the pain. No one tried to be terribly sympathetic with your pain. You just had to offer it up. When you put that mindset to sexuality, it's a hard pill to swallow. Part of my sexual awareness and sexual coming out happened in seminary. You can imagine the conflict of this happening among religious and spiritual people and knowing that it was not compatible with the very purpose for which I was there! Then being asked by my superiors at that time to be truthful which I was, they expelled me. They kicked me out.

Did you tell them that you were having feelings that you didn't understand or say that you were gay?

J: I explained that I'd had relationships with some of the men there. What it turned out to be was a mini witch-hunt and all of those people were expelled. I wasn't the only one. I was honest and hoping to find some guidance, but what I got instead was shown the door. Interestingly, years later, when I returned to that part of the country and went to a gay bar--guess who was there? It was my director of novices, which was a real eye-opening experience. I finished my college years in a Catholic college, but as each year went by I drifted further and further away even from worship. I felt that my sexuality and my faith were totally incompatible. There was no questioning the Catholic tradition and the Catholic faith--even those things that were unspoken. So, for the next several years, in college and eight years in New York, I rarely went to church. The only time was when I was with family, visiting, and it felt like such a hypocritical thing for me to do. Only after moving to San Francisco and finding a Catholic Church in the Castro that was composed of about seventy-five percent gay men, twenty percent elderly women and the rest families, right in the heart of the gay ghetto, did I find some comfort. When they preached from the pulpit, even though it was a Catholic message, it was a little bit more open. My partner at the time, Patrick, got sick. He had AIDS, and he died. When I went back to the church for comfort and counseling and solace, the priest I went to, a fine priest, could not acknowledge my relationship as anything more than a friendship. I was so repulsed by that, I never went back. I'd made some friends there, but those relationships ultimately were severed, because the hypocrisy reeked and I associated that with God. It wasn't until I found MCC that my feelings changed.

When my second partner, Gary, had HIV-related cancer and wanted to go to church, we tried the MCC Church. That was about 1995. That was the first time I went into a church and felt that I was honest with God. I didn't have to question who I was, my sexuality. I realized that the Catholic way was not the only way and that there was a roomful of people, hundreds of people just like me, who wanted nothing more than to be loved by God. I felt for the first time that I was loved just for who I was. That's not that long ago. Most of my life was lived feeling like I was different, but not in a good way. Now I know that I'm different, but in a very positive way, a way that is a gift. So that was an awakening which, of course, has led me on this very convoluted path that I certainly would not have predicted after being expelled from seminary in 1971, trying to answer what I felt was my first calling.

Joe, you were just starting to follow the path toward ministry for the second time when you and Eric met. Let's talk about that and then come back to your path toward ordination. How did you two meet?

J: Well, Gary died in 1997, and we had started coming to MCC before that. I was on disability at that time, because I also live with HIV. I was certain my life was going to be over. My health felt as if it was declining, although actually it wasn't. My body responded in a very positive way to the stress I was going through. Spiritually I was feeling very empty and lost. I kept praying to God to help me find a way, and I turned to the church, to MCC. I started just hanging out there during the day. I was in grief counseling there. I started volunteering for the church some, and then it became full time volunteering. I became the assistant to the senior pastor. It was during that time that I got my calling to MCC ministry. I had just started seminary in the fall of 1998 and was about to finish my first semester of schooling at the Pacific School of Religion. Part of my duty at the church was to participate in the food program there, the Simply Supper food program. I acted as one of the supervisors for the dining room to make sure it went smoothly. That's the first time that Eric and I met at lunch. Do you want to go on from here, Eric?

E: When I first moved to San Francisco I was working at A Different Light Bookstore which is a gay bookstore in the Castro. At that time the Simply Supper program at MCC was only happening on Wednesdays. The bookstore decided to provide volunteers and food so the church could serve meals on Wednesdays and Fridays. I actually started going to MCC through the food program. So, I was volunteering there through the bookstore. One of the days I was volunteering there, Joe's duty was to greet people at the door, the guests for the supper program. It was sort of one of those "across a crowded room" things. I saw him there, and I really recognized his gentle spirit first. I won't ever forget that, and I still see it. That's what first attracted me to him, plus the fact that he was pretty cute. So that's where we actually met. I suppose I'll tell the story that I've told many times over the last seven years. A side comment I need to insert here is that by the time I actually met Joe, I had changed jobs and was working in a restaurant in a hotel, but I was still volunteering at the program. There was another volunteer there whose name was Rodney, who also worked at the hotel. Anyway, I met Joe that day and had an instant crush on him. For some reason, our paths didn't cross again for a number of months, but sometime during the holidays or close to the beginning of the year, I volunteered at the church again, and Joe and I spoke again. The next day at work I asked Rodney about Joe, if he was single and so on. In the meantime, Joe had already asked Rodney at church if he knew anything about me, because he knew we worked together. So when I asked Rodney about Joe the next day at work he said, "Honey, I'm gonna make your New Year!" I guess you'd call it a mutual admiration society thing. That's how we met. It's really kind of nice when people ask us how we met to say, we met at church. It depends on who we talk to as to what kind of reaction we get.

J: I would agree that it is a neat feeling to say that we met at church, but I think the deeper level of that was that we met in a program at church that was about as Christian a program as you could offer, giving free, hot, delicious food to people, many of them homeless and living on the street, most of them living below the poverty level. Some may not have really needed that meal, but all were welcome in that space. I don't know if I believe in fate. I certainly don't believe that there is just one person out there for every individual. I will say that sometimes the Universe, God, the Creator, however you want to say it--I think there are just master strokes of design that enable people to open their hearts and open their eyes. I think all people have access to those moments, but so often we are disconnected because of the lives we live. We get into situations where we are so concerned with the practical that we forget the spiritual. We forget that in doing what I call God's work, which to me is looking out for our fellow human beings, the Spirit is working. When we aren't spending time doing that because we are so preoccupied with ourselves we shut off those other moments that really allow us to shine in our own radiance and the beauty that God created. I know when I first asked Rodney about Eric, I was certain Eric would not be interested in me, because I was a bit older, and it had only been a year and a half since Gary died. I was just starting a new calling, just starting seminary, and had a busy life ahead of me. I thought, "Who would want to spend their life with someone in training for the ministry, going through school?" When I asked Eric if he would want to go to dinner, he said he had planned to ask me. I can't tell you how surprised and delighted I was that the Universe had provided for me in that space. I think that we were both so open, partially because of the work we were doing there, that we saw a greater gift even beyond that. I think that would be true for most people. You know, when I counsel people who come to me with their troubles, the first thing I ask them is, "What are you doing for other people?" We get so caught up in self-service that we forget that there's a bigger issue out there. When we open ourselves to that issue wonderful things can fill our lives. That's what I think happened with us.

When you and Eric met at MCC, you had already resumed training to become an ordained minister. What called you back into that vocation after having left for a time?

J: It's interesting. I think "calling" is a very multi-faceted phenomenon. I think you are called by God. I think we call God. I think other people call you to things that you don't even see. While I was going to MCC after Gary's death and immersing myself, almost twenty/four-seven, in that church because I was in such deep grief, I needed to process it in some way. So, I offered it as work for the church, but my prayer to God was to open my heart, because I was in such pain. Open my heart and give me direction, because I can't see my own way. It came at a very unexpected time. In thinking back, from the moment I felt called, which was a very specific moment, by the way, others from the church had gotten to know me and asked me if I'd ever considered the ministry, saying I was good with people. My response was, "What, are you crazy? I work for these people!" I really didn't recall that until later. I happened to be facilitating an MCC conference for incoming clergy, and the person I worked for was one of the people on the faculty, which is why I was there. It was called an eight-day, intensive conference, because that was what it was, a very intense time of preparation. It was after that I had a couple of revelations during the week when it just hit me that this was what I was supposed to do. It was what I had been searching for my whole life. It totally caught me off guard, and yet, when I told others about it, they weren't surprised at all. I think that's what I meant earlier when I said we all have a calling, but it's only when you open yourself as wide as you can that you allow that calling to come to fruition without trying to manipulate it to what you want, but rather to listening to see perhaps what God wants it to be.

After you two dated and became a couple, there came a time in your relationship that you decided you wanted to do a commitment ceremony/ wedding to celebrate your love and commitment for each other. This, of course, is a controversial subject in our society and within most Christian denominations. Why was it important to you to have a wedding, as you prefer to call it? Why in the church?

J: Ours was clearly a wedding, and we are absolutely married. Many who's faith traditions frown on their relationships feel it's somehow disrespectful to call it by a traditional name, so they call it a holy union, or they don't even go that route and they do a civil ceremony. It is up to the individual, but as far as I'm concerned, by any stretch of the imagination, it is a marriage.

E: It wasn't a random choice to call it a wedding. It's like when I first came out. I sort of took it upon myself to educate people, not being afraid to be out and to say the word "gay", or "partner", or whatever. I learned early on that people aren't as afraid of that language as you think they'd be. As a result, I do refer to our wedding as a wedding. I bristle when people call Joe and me "boyfriends." A lot of times they don't know what else to say. I acknowledge that, but he's my husband. There's no question about it. It is choice for me to use that terminology. That's what it is, if society would just recognize it.

As a guest and participant, I felt it was a wedding, as well. I would guess that anyone who witnessed it felt the same way. Even though your wedding

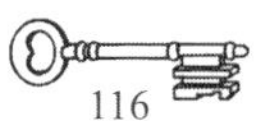

was a very special event, you also did a civil ceremony. Why do that in addition to the church wedding?

J: It's really the best of all worlds, in that we have about eight anniversaries. It's hard to keep track of them all.

E: The most legal thing we could do in San Francisco was to become domestic partners, which did afford us some legal rights. On February 14, 2000, we had a ceremony for domestic partnership at City Hall. A couple of friends of ours were witnesses, and it was really nice. That was our first anniversary and was as legal as we could get. Actually, our first anniversary was when we met, the second was our first date, and the domestic partnership was our third anniversary. Then in February of 2001, we had our wedding in the church. In February of 2004, for a brief time in San Francisco it became available for us to be legally married. It wasn't a mad rush to go down and do it, but we happened to have a fundraiser at church during that time, and there was a quartet singing in a talent show. Both couples in the quartet had been married that day at City Hall. Joe and I had been holding back to see what the legal ramifications of the whole deal were going to be before we decided to take advantage of the opportunity. There was such joy in the fact that these couples had been able to do this, and everyone was so happy for them, that Joe and I just looked at each other and knew we wanted to do it, too.

J: We discovered that they were going to keep City Hall open all weekend and that the mayor had made this proclamation. I told Eric that there was no time like the present. We planned to get up early the next day, which was the anniversary of our church wedding. We got down there and the lines were already forming. We waited for about two hours. There were literally hundreds and hundreds of couples lined up, and more were lined up for a week or two after that, before it was stopped by the courts.

E: We don't celebrate the anniversary of our annulment, but there's another sort of amusing anniversary.

J: It really wasn't an annulment, but it was voided. For a while they said that if we did the legal marriage, it would void the domestic partnership that we had established, but then the courts said the marriages were void, and domestic partnerships would remain intact.

E: It was as if it had never happened. That's why we have so many anniversaries, but we look forward to the day when we can celebrate our legal marriage.

J: I want to say one more word about that day when we got married in City Hall: There wasn't a church. One of my colleagues, also a minister, happened to be there to bless some of the weddings that day. Actually, she and her partner were witnesses for us. I just want to say that although we loved our wedding, and it was great to have our families and friends there to support us, love us, and treat us just like we deserved to be treated--and they wanted to treat us well and celebrate our love--that ceremony in City Hall was almost more moving. Here we were in the public square, so to speak, being recognized by a public official, and being celebrated. It was very quick. We didn't spend nearly as much money as we did for the wedding, and yet, it was equally meaningful because of the symbols of what was behind it. God was just as present there as in the church. We knew when we told our families and friends that they would be delighted for us. The moment was just as emotional for me, because it was a moment that was long overdue. For the first time I truly felt like a full citizen. It didn't last as long as we would have liked, but it will come again.

Are there things about the church wedding you would like to revisit?

E: I'll say that I used to sort of roll my eyes when people said that their wedding day was the most beautiful day of their life, but now I understand what they were talking about. It will always be such a wonderful memory. We took on a lot that weekend. Since we were having family come in from out of town for the wedding on Saturday, we scheduled Joe's ordination service on that Sunday. Having our wedding on Saturday and Joe's being ordained as an MCC minister on Sunday made it quite an emotional and full of milestones weekend. Another point of interest was that the senior pastor, Penny, who would be officiating at the wedding, got a phone call from a documentary company out of London that was making a documentary about the Catholic Church and homosexuality. They were looking for a gay wedding to film, and she told them that ours was coming up. We actually had a very positive experience with them being at our wedding. Put together a wedding, an ordination, and a film crew following us around, and we had quite a wonderful weekend. Along with all of that, we had family from out of town. I was talking earlier about the community at MCC and how important that became. That was one of the reasons we had a wedding--to have those we love around to sort of affirm and confirm our love in the presence of God--invoking that Spirit, as well. That's what a wedding is to me, and that's exactly how ours played out. It was the first time Joe's and my families had met, and that was really nice. It really was one of the most special days of my life.

You were very intentional in your planning to include family in the rituals of the wedding. You might talk a little about that in light of the fact that so many MCC members don't have the support of their families in their lives.

J: We both grew up in very strong Midwestern families that are close families. We were very clear that we wanted the mingling of our lives to be a continuation of the way that families have mingled for centuries. We very intentionally created a ritual whereby a candle was passed between family members, and then candles on the altar were lit to symbolize the joining of not only our two lives, the histories and traditions of our two lives, but for a new family and a new tradition. It was a very moving part of the service for us, although we all laughed when I had to remind Eric about the hugging. We had agreed that after this ritual we would not only greet our own families, but to also greet our new families. As in most weddings, there was a hitch--the candle Eric and I were supposed to light was missing, but we faked it, and it worked out fine.

E: That kind of brings me back to my earlier conversation about creating ritual. That was a ritual that we created. Joe wrote the text for it, and together we orchestrated it. It was a very important symbol that we created. That's one of the things that I learned from Rebecca back in Oregon--how important ritual can be.

J: Ritual really is the embodiment of the practice of life. It embodies symbolically the way you want things to be, or the way that they have been. That's true of dance in ritual or ceremony. It's true of everything. That's why we were so intentional about that ritual in our wedding, not only the way we wanted it to be, but also the way we would choose to live it out. Fortunately, we have followed up with that by respecting and loving each other's families. After all, we are an extension of our families of origin, and we are a new family. That's the way it's been for centuries, and that's how we decided to embody it.

You both have theater background. Do you think this might have something to do with your being connected to ritual? Is this why you are moved to "act out," so to speak, the important events and emotions in your lives?

E: I think that there is, at times, a very fine line between theater and church, and I mean that in a good way. It's about finding different ways to express a connection to God. So, yes, I definitely think our theater backgrounds play a part in how we create worship.

J: I would clarify that for myself and say "drama," my drama background, because I used to bristle when people would raise the specter of theater as opposed to church--how preaching should be easy for me, because I used to be an actor. It's a totally different thing, because in theater the words and direction are someone else's. In preaching and in ritual, they are words that you've prepared, so they come from your heart, and it's done in a very, very different way. Sure, practice in delivery and your speaking voice and all of that comes in handy, but if you don't ever grasp that in a natural way, then you're sunk either as an actor or a preacher, because it's really, really important. That kind of takes care of itself. I think the rituals that we created showed in a dramatic way the real feeling, devotion and love we have, not only for each other, but for our families. I think that's why it came out. Our theater background helped us to create it, but it was purely from the heart.

We have talked a lot about MCC church, but many people might not know what that is and how it came to be. How are your congregations different from the mainstream denominations?

J: Back in 1968, a man by the name of Troy Perry, who was a gay man and a Baptist minister, was rejected not only by his family, but also by his church. He felt there needed to be a place--and I might say here that queer community was not as inclusive as it is now, so the terminology then was centered mainly on gays and lesbians. Now it's bisexual, transgender, intersexed, queer, questioning--all the words now that we use to be as inclusive as we can. He wanted to create an opportunity for gays and lesbians who had been rejected as he had been by the mainstream churches to find a place where they could come and worship just like everyone else. A place where they could openly honor God and their beliefs in an organized, liturgical way as a temporary measure, until the mainstream churches came to their senses in ten or twenty years and welcomed gays and lesbians into their congregations, as God welcomes them and celebrates them. That ten to twenty year experiment has become a permanent fixture because, unfortunately, the majority of the mainstream churches have not come to their senses. In fact, many are ready to split over this issue. So, MCC Church started in 1968 with a dozen people in Troy Perry's living room, celebrating and worshiping God. Now there are several hundred churches worldwide, tens of thousands of members in MCC Churches.

E: Some people think of it as a non-denominational church when you talk about your involvement there. The denomination is actually Metropolitan Community Church.

J: It's true, and a lot of people think a non-denominational church just springs up out of nothing in the middle of nowhere. Although we are congregation-led, meaning we are community-led, the power rests with the congregation. We do have the Fellowship as an umbrella organization, so in that regard we are a denomination. We often find ourselves as a potpourri of many Christian backgrounds. I would say that the majority of our members are from Roman Catholic or Baptist backgrounds. Then there is quite a healthy mix of other Christian backgrounds and even some other faith traditions. These are people who are drawn to the church just as in days of old, for its community aspects, not necessarily because of what it says it believes. We are a non-creedal church, meaning we don't have a creed that you have to subscribe to in order to become a member or to participate. That's a very personal and private thing.

I know you had a number of outreach ministries at your former MCC Church in San Francisco. Just recently you have moved to a place where you, Joe, are senior pastor and, Eric, you are an active member. People might think all you do at your church is talk about gay and lesbian issues. Fill us in on what ministry in your church looks like.

J: It's kind of a double-handed ministry, because the fact is that queer people are still marginalized, both in culture and in religion. That makes it a constant and recurring issue that can't just be shoved aside to say now we are mainstream, so we can concentrate on other things. Having said that, however, when that becomes the focus, we lose sight of the greater mission, the social gospel of Jesus, which was inclusion of all of God's people. So, it's not just doing ministry for queer people. That's why we have straight people, as well, who come to our church. They are there, not because they see us as a gay church, but because they hear the message. There are many opportunities to serve the community, and that's what makes it a community church. We pay attention to the church in the area where it is located and in global areas, as well. Our church here in Gainesville is not a large church, so we don't have a lot of resources, but most recently, we responded to Hurricane Katrina. Many people have been relocated here, so we collected food and clothing and made sure that got distributed. We have a partnership with the Gainesville Area AIDS Project. We provide meals every month for that. We have a Deacon's Pantry that provides food for anyone who is in need of it. We have moneys set aside for people who are having difficulties, like losing a job. We might help them pay some of their bills. We have an outreach ministry to the students at the University of Florida. We are just now starting to grow some of our own ministries, like a children's program in our congregation. So, our reach is far beyond the perimeters of the church boundaries. The more we are in the community and see the needs of the community, the more we can respond. Recently, there was a peace march. Some of the people in the church participated in that. That was sponsored by a lot of other churches. I am already involved in a few interfaith organizations here in Gainesville. That's another opportunity for our voice to blend with other voices in the greater faith community, especially in the areas of peace and justice.

Eric, in a conversation several of us had recently, it was brought up that you had the opportunity to find a calling or ministry to meaningful work in your position at MCC San Francisco and in your search for work after your move to this new place. Will you address that comment?

E: Before we moved here, I worked at MCC San Francisco as an office manager. One of the things that came up in the conversation was that part of my position was as a sort of greeter. I was the first person people dealt with as they came in to the offices of the church. Sometimes they were people who came upstairs to participate in our food program and other times they were guests visiting San Francisco who just wanted to check out the church. I don't quite know how to explain it as a ministry, but like Joe was saying earlier, I just tried to be open--to open my heart to whoever came up the stairs. One of the things I constantly remind myself of--and I don't really think of it as a ministry with a capital M--but whenever I pray with people or relate to people, I try to see God's face in every face I encounter. I certainly have to keep reminding myself of that, but I try to keep an open heart with people. There's a Buddhist term called "right livelihood"--it's a term that has stuck with me. It is usually one of my objectives on a resume, to find a right livelihood. I was fortunate to get a job in Gainesville as office manager of a Ronald McDonald House, which provides housing for parents who have sick children in the hospital. Because a person spends so much time at work, it seems important to me to be helping people in the process. Part of that inclination has to do with the way I was raised. I guess you could call that a ministry.

Are there any stories or scriptures that you want to finish up with? Do you have any hopes or dreams for the future that you want to put out there?

J: I think if there is one scripture that pops out at me--it doesn't apply specifically to the queer community, but to any marginalized people--it's from the Gospel of John. Jesus and the disciples encountered a man who was born blind. The disciples asked Jesus who had sinned--the man, or his parents--that he was born blind. There was clearly a very deeply rooted belief in retribution theology, that God punishes people based on either something they've done or something the parents did. Jesus sums it up by saying,

"Neither this man nor his parents has sinned. He was born blind that God's works might be revealed through him." I think that's true of all people. It's very easy for us to feel guilty. Both the Catholic faith, the Jewish faith are riddled with guilt, as are other faith traditions. I think that operating from this fear mentality turns us away from God, not toward God. If it does turn us toward God it is trembling with fear. Fear and love just cannot go together. I always go to that scripture and always believe that Jesus was the Enlightened Being that everyone says, because he is able to see and teach in a way that was neither black nor white, but transcendent, realizing that God works in mysterious ways far beyond our knowing. That's why that scripture resonates so for me, and it applies to everything.

E: Oftentimes people's experience when they first come to an MCC Church is to weep, and I was reminded of this recently when a friend of mine from work came. I didn't even know him that well, but I had invited him, and he came. When he saw all kinds of people, gay couples, straight couples, families coming up to communion and putting the communion bread into each other's mouths, it was very moving to him. I think that often comes from the realization that people see that they can be gay and God can love them--they can go to church and be gay at the same time. So many gay people have heard years of messages opposite from that. I guess if I want to leave anything with anyone, it's that God loves you no matter what. That's often an underlying message at MCC Church, and sometimes I take that for granted because I was raised to believe that. I sometimes forget there are people who are really struggling with that, so that's what I want them to hear.

Kate and Sara

Centered in Christ

I first noticed Kate and Sara slipping in and out of the early church service on Sunday mornings several years ago. They were attending regularly, but seemed not to want to stand out in the crowd. I had a feeling that they might be a "couple," and didn't want attention drawn to themselves. If they were gay, I could understand their reluctance to be viewed with curiosity, or worse.

I hoped that if they were a couple they would find a church home with us. My dream was for folks in the gay and lesbian community to have a safe place to be accepted, to grow spiritually, and to use their gifts and graces.

When I finally had a chance to meet them, my intuition told me I was right. As time went on, there was more evidence that their presence was going to provide a unique situation for our congregation to experience and a wonderful opportunity for us to grow in faith--Sara was pregnant!

After a brief time of adjustment, Kate and Sara became active on one of the church committees. They chose to work together on the same committee. I assumed that they felt more comfortable sticking together.

Six years from the time they started attending Trinity, we did this interview.

Kate, tell me about your growing-up years. Were you involved in a church and, if so, how was that experience?

Kate: Well, our family didn't go to church at all, but when I was in the third grade, my brothers went to Vacation Bible School. They had gone all week. It was Friday, the last day, and they were going to this picnic at the park. I was crushed because I wasn't going to be allowed to go to the picnic with my brothers. Then the pastor, Wendell Rovenstein, I love him to this day, said, "Sure

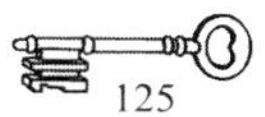

she can go." So I went to the picnic and started going to church. My brothers never went back. They had just gone because they knew the pastor's son. I started going to church then, and went until I was a junior in high school. I never missed a Sunday. It was just me. I walked to church every Sunday. There was this guy with three kids who stopped and gave me a ride when I was halfway there each week.

I stopped going when I was a junior in high school, because I got a job and had to work a lot of Sundays. I just kind of fell away from church, but never away from God. I didn't get back to church until about six years ago, after Sara and I got together. We'd been together for five years before that. Even before we started back to church, we read "The Daily Bread" and "The Upper Room" every morning, faithfully. I couldn't bring myself to go to church. I just felt weird about it. I wasn't sure how we'd be accepted. I just wasn't comfortable.

One morning after I'd gone to work, Sara had continued to read devotions. She called me at work and told me about this fellow who kept saying he'd go back to church someday. He kept saying that, and when he finally made it back it was for his own funeral.

That story was what we needed to get going. Sara started making some calls to churches until she got hold of Pastor John, and we started going to our present church.

Sara, what did he say that made you feel like it would be okay to go to Trinity?

Sara: It was hard for me to ask what church you could go to if you were gay, but I did, and he got all excited and said, "Oh, come to Trinity." He just popped off and said, "Come on." I thought, "Wow! Okay, then!" That was six years ago.

How was it when you actually came to church that first Sunday? Were you comfortable?

K: We were scared to death, but we went, and the youth did the whole service. I knew Brian, the youth director, from college. Sara and I just thought, "Wow!" It was wonderful. We loved it. We sat in the same spot we sit in now, six years later. The people who sit around us have just been wonderful. We didn't know names at first, but we just sort of fell into place. Over time, people started visiting with us, and we wouldn't sit anywhere else now.

Were you pregnant then?

S: Oh no! Pastor John was the first person we talked to about it, though. I hadn't even talked to my parents about it yet. I wanted to get someone else's opinion before I did it. He said, "Yeah! Go for it!"

I hadn't talked to my parents about how they would feel if we had a kid. I went to him and said, "This is what we want to do." We didn't know if it was a good thing or a bad thing or how it would turn out, but he just kept saying, "Go for it! There's no better thing than two loving parents."

That's great!

K: We had a set of ideas about how we wanted to proceed. We wanted to talk to both folks, her folks and my mom and John before we did anything. We had some friends who had a baby and went through the same kind of process with the donors and the clinics like we were thinking about. When we told our parents, everyone was excited. Their response was, "Please do!" Her mom went to WalMart immediately and bought some baby things.

Our one disappointment was that John was eventually re-appointed to another church, so he wasn't there to baptize Faith.

How long have you been together?

K: Eleven years in March. We talked about having a baby for five years before we did anything about it.

How did you decide who would get pregnant?

K: My mother told me when I was very young that when you're pregnant you have one foot in the grave. I said, "That's it! I'm not doing it."

S: She was scared to death!

K: Well, it was because of my birth. I was breech, and there were lots of problems with the delivery. At one point they didn't think either of us was going to make it. I've been petrified ever since I heard that story, so I told Sara she could do it--she was younger.

Lets take a minute to talk about your faith background, Sara. Did you grow up going to church?

S: Yeah, I grew up Catholic.

Are your folks still Catholic?

S: Actually, they just started going back to church.

Do you think you influenced them in that direction?

S: I hope so. They started having a lot of medical problems, too. When I was growing up my dad only went to church with us on holidays. He's Protestant.

Sara, tell me about your siblings.

S: Well, I have one brother and one sister. My brother lives with us right now and my sister lives out of state.

How have your parents dealt with your being gay? Have they pretty much accepted it?

K: Well, actually, not really. I didn't tell my family right off the bat.

S: I don't think you ever did tell your family, did you?

K: Not really, my dad basically found out. One night he was at one of the local drinking establishments having a few liquors when he saw a friend of mine that I played ball with, and he just flat-out asked her. I guess he had his suspicions. So from then on he blabbed it here and there. My brothers just kind of figured it out from everyone else. My mom never really talks about it. She loves Sara and calls her her daughter. She's made that very clear, and Faith is her granddaughter. Faith is the one grandchild who has the dark hair and dark eyes that she loves. She treats us the same as anybody else. We just don't talk about it. My two brothers kid me about it. We'll be doing something and they'll make some crack about it, but they don't really care. They really do love me. We've always kind of stuck together. Then I have a half-sister, but she's not really around.

You said that church is really important to you. What keeps you coming back, Sunday after Sunday? What would you say is the draw?

K: I guess from the time I was sixteen until I was twenty-one, I was pretty wild. I had a lot of fun, of course--I'm not going to lie to you. I really wasn't a bad person--I was just doing what a lot of kids do--drinking and partying. But, all along--and I think this was the Holy Spirit--there was just this knocking and saying, "You need to get your act together."

When I was twenty-one I was playing ball in a tournament, and I broke my leg. I don't know how to put this--I just think God talks to you if you'll listen. I felt like God was telling me that this was my "wake-up" call and a second chance. I didn't start back to church, but I've always been a Christian.

At this time, I was in a relationship, my first relationship with a woman--well, if you don't count the one in the fifth grade. Really, I had a girlfriend in the fifth grade, a sixth grader. Anyway, this was when I was twenty-four and I met this girl who was eighteen, and she was my first relationship.

We moved to a college town and were going to school. As it turned out, she was abusive--very abusive, both physically and mentally. So I called this friend of mine from high school, my best friend. I was upset and crying, and I was talking to her. She said that I needed to tell her what was going on, to just say it. So I did. I said, "I'm gay."

My friend said, "Okay, now, I want you to go get your Bible and start reading it."

I did what she said to do. I went and got my Bible and I started reading it. As I read I just kept getting closer and closer to God. This was in about 1987. What was ironic about that whole deal was that when I was in high school, this friend was the person who talked me out of staying in the church and pulled me away from my involvement! Now, God was using her to pull me back in.

How did that play itself out? What did you do to "get back into it?"

K: I made a promise that I was going to read the Bible, so I sat down that summer and I read the whole Bible. Every night I read as much as I could until I was done and then I started buying other books. I was having trouble with the stuff in the Bible that was negative--the place where it talks about two same-sex people together being an abomination, that you shouldn't do this, and you shouldn't do that I started to think I was wrong. That's when my friend bought me the book, *Good News for Modern Gays*. After I read that book I thought, "Okay, I'm all right."

How long did your struggle with Scripture before you could be at peace with what the Bible said, and with who you were?

K: It was probably about six months. I wanted to do what God wanted me to do, but I wanted to be myself. It was then that I broke off my not-so-healthy relationship and soon met Sara. I felt like I was a pretty strong Christian by then. Eventually, we started going to church, and together we just kept getting better. I could see her growing, too.

We talked before the interview started about favorite scriptures that support and guide you in your life. Yours was Jeremiah 29:11-12, "For I know the plans I have for you" says the Lord, "plans for welfare and not for evil, to give you a future and a hope." That seems to have been especially true when you and Sara began your life together.

K: Well, it just gives me order and comfort in my life. I know God has a plan for my life, and it will unfold as it is supposed to if I trust God and listen for Him in my life. Sara and Faith are proof of the good that comes out of that.

Sara, you said that you grew up Catholic. Did you go to church nearly every Sunday?

S: We went to church every Sunday and CCD every Wednesday night. It was that way until I was out of high school. We got baptized and went through confirmation and all that.

My parents were married and divorced and re-married and divorced and now living together. The church shunned us because of the divorce, and then I kept hearing it was a sin to be gay. Once you figure out that you are gay, and you are in that condemning environment, it's not good. I didn't feel accepted at all.

Did you feel okay about being gay, but not interested in the church any more, or did what you heard from the pulpit affect you?

S: I felt okay but lost. It's hard when you're told you're wrong.

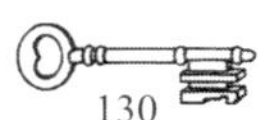

Did you actually have a conversation with your folks when you told them you were gay?

S: No! No! Actually, a letter went to my parents' home. My mom claimed it was open and she read it. Then she knew I was gay. She called me at college and told me to come home. My dad threatened to lock me in the basement until I was ninety-nine. I shed a lot of tears that day--a lot of tears.

So where did it go from there? Did it get better?

S: It gradually got better. I did some counseling. I was in counseling a lot. My dad was an alcoholic, so we went to Alateens and all that stuff. I did some more counseling in college, because I was really messed up after my parents found out I was gay. My counselor actually recommended that my parents come to one of my sessions. My mom did, and she said that she didn't really have a problem with it. She just needed to quit beating herself up over it. From then on it got so much better.

When did you two meet and start your relationship?

K: Actually, Sara was in her last year of college. We had met several years before that when we were playing in a ball tournament. We were sitting on the bench together because I was old, and she wasn't any good at it. Just kidding. I'm actually twelve years older than Sara. Anyway, we were just sitting at the end of the bench talking and ended up having a really fun day together. I was at the end of another relationship and she was in and out of relationships.

S: I was going to school in another town, but I'd see Kate off and on at the grocery store or somewhere else, and I'd say, "Hi!"

K: She'd go out of her way to be nice and friendly. I like to say she was the pursuer! So one weekend my roommates and I had a party at our house. It was the weekend of the Big Eight Women's Basketball Tournament. Sara was on spring break, so she came to the party and then went out to California to visit her sister the rest of the time. When she got back in town, she called me. We went out, and we've been together ever since. That was in March, 1993. It's been good. It's been really good.

Do you think the fact that you have had a faith connection has helped solidify the relationship?

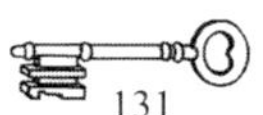

K: Absolutely. Everything is centered on Christ, and we talk about that a lot. Our family, Sara, Faith and I, and now Sara's brother, are all centered on Christ. That's just the way we are.

S: It wouldn't work otherwise, because you have so many struggles. It would be too easy to fall apart--too easy not do the work.

K: I have my times when I'm bothered and she has her times when she's bothered. In those times, either she's the one who is encouraging me or I'm encouraging her. We'll say, "Let's just find our faith, or let's just pray about it." We had something come up last week and decided to pray about it. We'd no more than walked in the house and we'd received our blessing. It works for us and helps us to be strong. Faith is a wonderfully spiritual child--very shy, but very spiritual. We sit together at our meals and pray. Faith asks the blessing. When we go to bed at night, we pray. We each say a prayer and then we say one together.

S: One night she said, "Mom, you stay here. I have to go in the bathroom to say a prayer, but I don't want you to hear it." She prays for her toys and things that are important to her. She prays for her little friend who's having seizures. Every night she prays, "God bless my friend and her seizures."

Before the interview started, you shared your favorite Scripture with me and said having a child made it especially meaningful to you. It was John 3:16, "For God so loved the world that he sent his only Son, that whoever believes in him should not perish but have eternal life." Explain your feelings on that in relation to Faith.

S: Having a child whom I love so much helps me understand how much God loves us--to send Him to die for us. He had to love his Son as much as I love my child. It was such an amazing sacrifice.

Many churches, United Methodist and numerous others, are reluctant to ordain ministers who are openly gay. They won't allow pastors in their local congregations to perform holy unions. Do you have any comments about that? How does that affect you?

S: I'm scared to death of Baptists! I don't want to say they hate, but it doesn't seem like love!

K: We, for one, have really never needed to have a ceremony or get married. It's just not something we want to do. It's not that we aren't committed because we totally are. We've had too many friends who have gone that route and, since it isn't legal, it's too easy to just get in and get out. We don't need it to be committed.

I don't like the fact that all those states just voted to ban it. It's not a bad thing. It can bring about some good. For instance, I was finally able to get the girls on my insurance at work. I pay a little more to do that but at least I can. My company has a domestic partnership program available. It helps, but I pay a lot more than a straight spouse for the same advantages. The marriage thing might push some of those benefits forward.

You had to do extra legal work with a lawyer to get other benefits that are automatic with a straight couple, right?

K: Yes. We had to be very specific about things. It isn't automatic just because we're a couple. We actually went prior to having Faith. We had our wills and our powers of attorney taken care of--plus our living wills. Then, after we had Faith, we went back and named me legal guardian so I could get insurance on her. We had our wills changed to make sure that Faith was taken care of or if something happened to either of us, Faith would stay with the other. We didn't want to take any chances. Sometimes things happen and you have to fight for them. We didn't want that to happen.

Are you considering having another child?

S: If we strike it rich! It's so expensive and insurance won't pay for it. We just saved for it the first time and paid for it out of pocket. Actually, the clinic where we went before won't even do in vitro for single women any more.

K: It's interesting we'd said we'd try the procedure to get pregnant up to three times. Sara was heartbroken when it didn't happen the third time and was discouraged about doing it again. I said, "Let's just try it one more time."

S: This friend of ours printed up a list of scriptures for encouragement. "Ask and it shall be given," "Where two or more are gathered in my name," and some others.

K: So we read the scriptures, and she and our friend and I prayed. After the fourth try, I was just so psyched. On the way home I just prayed for God to show me a sign. I saw a race car go by on a trailer and it had my lucky number on it. I said to myself, "You know what, we're pregnant."

S: We went in just before Christmas on the 17th of December and found out New Years Day.

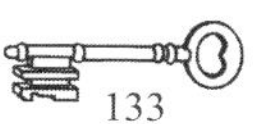

K: We found out together and we cried---and we laughed--and we went out to Target and bought a little bear. It was neat and we would do it again, but it would need to be soon. Age becomes a factor.

Tell me about getting Faith baptized. Was that uncomfortable to be in front of the congregation?

S: Special and scary. She actually wore the gown my grandfather was baptized in. Then it was used for all the kids and grandkids. We were lucky enough to be able to have Faith baptized in it just like I was. We didn't know quite how to do it, though. We didn't know if all three of us should stand up there in front of everybody in the church.

K: We didn't want to stand out or offend anybody in the church, but we felt like Faith had a right to be baptized in that church, too. We went to talk to Pastor Susan to see what she would say. Again, we were nervous because, we had started this with Pastor John, so we hadn't done anything about it yet. We were out in the hall talking to one of the other church staff, and she just popped out with it. "Kate and Sara have something they want to talk to you about."

S: "Oh no! Not yet!" It was all right, though.

K: We went ahead and told Pastor Susan that we were expecting and that we wanted to have the baby baptized. She was wonderful.

S: We actually had both our families stand up with us, so we weren't alone. We stood up with my brother, my sister and Kate's mom.

K: Pastor said that this was what it was all about--family. As it turns out, Faith has been a star since she's been there. Everybody in that church who knows us loves her. We've had people say, "We can't wait to see what she's going to do at children's time." They watch to see what she's going to wear. It's kind of funny. She's very feminine and wants to wear dresses and lace. They really love her and that makes it so much easier.

S: One of our dilemmas now is what to do about church directory pictures. We are kind of uncomfortable with all three being in the same picture. We will probably each take separate pictures with Faith. We don't want to make a fuss. The people who know us are really wonderful to us, but we don't know how people who don't know us feel. We'll probably continue to try to blend in like everyone else. We're not out to make any big statement. We're just glad to have a church where we can feel safe and grow in our relationship with God.

After the tape had run its course and we assumed the interview was over, we sat at the dining room table and started telling stories. One of the faith stories that Kate told touched my heart. I wanted to share it as part of this couple's interview.

K: This is my story that I call "Wet Pants." We talked a little bit earlier about the fact that if you listen, God talks to you. One of the times God nudges me is when I'm really busy, running here and running there. One of those times was when I was running to my mom's. I was driving there on my way home from work. From a distance, I noticed a girl walking down the sidewalk in my direction. As she got closer I could see that she had some problems. She was probably mentally challenged. It was a really hot day and she had on a pair of jeans. When I took a closer look it was obvious she had wet her pants. I was in a hurry, but I kept feeling like God was telling me I needed to stop and help this girl. I knew I should pull over, but I just had to get to Mom's and get the things done I needed to do. In my mind, I kept beating myself up, knowing I should have stopped. I said, "Okay, God, next time I feel you nudging me, I promise I'll stop."

A couple of weeks later, Sara and I had gone over to some friends' house to play cards and games. We stayed until around eleven. At that time, we lived in a trailer park. When we got home I parked in front of the trailer, next to her pick-up. Sara walked up the sidewalk and onto the porch and was standing there because she had her hands full. I got my stuff out of my truck and was going around Sara's truck to go in, when this fellow jumped out from behind her vehicle and came towards me, yelling. "Hey!"

Sara is still on the porch and I'm startled and jump back. He starts coming towards me, not really threatening, still scary. I kept backing up, finally getting behind a small tree we'd planted. Sara's screaming for me to get up on the porch, I'm yelling for him to stay back, and he's yelling that he needs a ride someplace.

The interesting thing about all this is that when I'm scared, I get a sharp pain in my stomach, a fear pain. I realized that I didn't have that pain, so I finally yell back at this guy, "All right! Do you have any guns or knives?" "No, no! I don't!"

I told him that he needed to go lie down in the back of my truck. Sara, even though she was scared to death, got in the front with me. He tells me what the address is where he wants to go, but when we get there it's not a valid address. We drive on a few blocks to a lighted parking lot and I ask Sara to get his driver's license through a crack in the window. I looked at the address on the license and began to drive across town where this address was. When we got there he jumps out of the truck and comes over to my window. I rolled it down and I realized he was trying to stick his head in there and give me a hug. So, anyway, he said he just wanted to thank me. When I got a closer look, I realized that he was covered with tattoos, and his head was shaved. He looked like a "skinhead." I told him that he didn't need to thank me--he needed to thank Jesus because that was the reason I did this.

He then proceeded to tell me that he was a Christian and believed in God. He told me that he was going into the service the next day and had gone out with some friends.

They'd gotten kind of drunk and they had just dumped him off. He'd started walking and had ended up at our house. I don't think that was an accident.

So, I said to him, "God Bless." And we came on home. The reason I call this story "Wet Pants" is because I hadn't helped that girl with wet pants. The night we picked this kid up, it was raining and when he walked away from my truck, all he had on was soaking wet blue jeans.

* *

When it came time to have the Church directory family pictures taken, Sara and Kate decided to have separate pictures made with Faith. The lady who was shooting the photographs made no comment when Sara came in with Faith, but when Kate followed, bringing Faith in for a second photo session, the photographer began to question her. She wanted to know why the child was getting her photo done twice. She questioned Kate's relationship with Faith, saying that she had called Sara Mommy. She wanted to know if they were trying to get an extra set of photos of the child somehow. After much discussion, the photographer gave in and kept the appointment with Kate and Faith.

In the room where proofs were being reviewed and final selections made, both for purchase and for a complimentary 8x10 portrait, the questioning started all over again. The saleswoman wanted to make sure they knew that they would only get one free photograph. They would have to choose which adult was in the photo but they couldn't do both.

Finally, the minister caught wind of what was going on and entered the room. He told the salesperson that these ladies were part of our church family and, if they couldn't be treated with respect, the entire church's order would be cancelled and another company hired to do the directory. The ladies got their photographs, but not without the fuss they had hoped to avoid.

Brian S.

Angel Unaware

I first met Brian when I was working in the bookstore at a small United Methodist college. Both of my young adult offspring were off to college, and I found that being around college students filled my "empty nest." Although most college-aged people would not readily admit that they might still need a little mothering, I suspect my attempts to show concern and support through their daily struggles and triumphs might have filled a void for them, also.

Brian was a student who was active in many areas of student life. He participated in music, theater, political life and student social activities. He was in and out of the bookstore, picking up poster paper, markers and other supplies. He was friendly and always willing to chat for awhile. His easy chuckle always set the stage for an upbeat conversation.

My intuition told me there was a possibility that Brian was gay, but I didn't know that for sure. I can't really remember how or when that fact was confirmed, but eventually I knew it to be true. After Brian graduated from college, I lost track of him for a number of years, never suspecting that he would end up being a significant person in my life and in my faith journey.

When I decided to write a book of stories about the faith journeys of homosexual persons in the United Methodist Church, I knew Brian's story had to be told. I met him at his office, from which he served as Conference Youth Coordinator for our United Methodist Conference. We went out for lunch and then returned to his office for this interview.

What was your church like when you were growing up, Brian?

Brian: I grew up in a small church in the Midwest. I guess I never heard anything preached from the pulpit on homosexuality, either positive or negative. It was just never mentioned. It wasn't until later that I experienced some of the different issues from the Church.

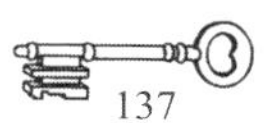

Was that after you left home?

No, it was probably when I got to middle school or high school. I began to hear kids talk more about fag this and fag that. I remember going to a small town revival with a friend and hearing about the different sins, and homosexuality was one of those that came up. I'm not even sure that I had put myself into that category yet, but I did know that I had some attraction for the same sex. That was probably the start of my struggle with what and who I was--what that meant to be in the church.

Did you ever have a conflict, thinking that you might not be able to be gay and a Christian? Did you think you might have to give up your faith?

Oh, yeah. I questioned why God would make me this way--a way that I thought was a big sin. When I got out of high school I quit going to church until probably my sophomore or junior year in college. I couldn't reconcile having this sin and being in the church.

Did you have issues with other sins in your life like the old standards of smoking and drinking? Did you feel bad about yourself for sin in general?

I guess, really, homosexuality was the big one. I was a nerd in high school, probably still am a nerd. I did a little partying in college, but I didn't smoke or do drugs. I guess that's why the homosexuality thing was such a big deal for me.

So when you went to college, did you find other gay students or were you pretty much in the closet and alone?

I guess that the first two years in college I was pretty much in the closet. I never said to anyone that I was gay, and then in about my junior year, I had a meltdown. I ended up leaving school, leaving home and driving to Nashville, Tennessee. After a couple of weeks of reflection, I knew that I was going to have to accept this and be who I was or it was going to end up killing me. No one knew where I was. I did let my parents know that I was okay, but didn't tell them what was going on.

When I got back home, I sat down and wrote a letter to my parents, letting them know what I was dealing with--that I was gay--that this was who I was. I dealt with them, and then started telling trusted friends at school that I was gay. From that time on, I never had a negative experience. It wasn't easy for my parents to deal with, but they had always showed me unconditional love, so there was never any thought that they weren't going to love me or that I wasn't going to be a part of the family. Most of my friends, when I told them, said, "Well, duh!" But, even at that, they were very supportive.

I know you were very active on campus when you were in college. Do you think that was because you liked to be active, or was it maybe an effort to compensate?

I'm sure there's an overcompensation issue even with what I do today. Knowing that people know that I'm gay, I want them to see that I'm no different than anyone else, and maybe I do try to achieve more. I'm sure that had some part in it then, too.

Tell me again what area your degree is in.

My degree is in music and theater education.

Was being part of United Methodist College a help or a hindrance, or did it even make any difference?

Like when I was having my meltdown? Really, I came back to school and finished out my semester. I had instructors that I told and friends that I told. Even though it was a United Methodist school, I found that staff and instructors were very supportive. I do still struggle, though, with the fact that there is no sort of support for gay students. I hope that changes someday.

Was there a turning point in your life when you knew that who you were could fit with your faith journey?

I grew up in the United Methodist Church, so I always had a connection with the Church. After I graduated from college, I went to work for the Larned Correctional Mental Health Facility, a state prison program. At that time I had the opportunity to work with people who had been in trouble. It was then that I realized that, with my degree in education, I could work with youth on the other end and possibly help prevent them from ever getting there. Having had a connection to the church my whole life, and wanting to be a part of a local church, I can see now that those two things merged. I think what happened next was a "God thing."

My job, being a government position, was eliminated when funding ran out.

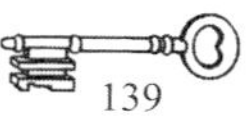

My position was cut, so I moved back home and was working at a department store, selling suits. One day a friend came in the store and told me that her church was looking for a youth director. She said she thought of me and wondered if I would consider applying.

I thought about it and prayed about it and ended up sending in my resume. I was called for interviews with the pastor, the Staff-Parish Committee and finally, the youth. At the time it seemed like a long interview process, but each time I went another step with it I felt more strongly that this was what I was being called to do.

I know that you leveled with John, the minister at the time, about your sexuality, and that he said he didn't see any problem with that. He said that all the staff was expected to adhere to an appropriate set of values, and that he expected the same from you.

Oh, sure. I've always felt that no matter if people are gay or straight, we have to have the same respect for ourselves. I intended to bring that to the youth in my ministry. My goals for them were spiritual growth, great fellowship and learning accountability.

Trinity United Methodist Church was where your church home was for five years as youth director. Did you find that your time there helped with your faith journey? Did it do anything to help reconcile your faith and your sexuality?

Oh, yes! Trinity was a big part of my journey into being and understanding who I was. There were people, in addition to my parents, who helped me understand unconditional love. These were families who I was out to, who knew everything about me, and it wasn't a big deal. I was a part of their family activities, and that was very affirming to me. They totally trusted me with their youth. That helped me a lot.

Brian, I'm asking everyone what Scripture sustains them in their daily lives. What's yours?

Hmmm, I don't know of one. It kind of depends on the day. Let me think about it. Everyone will probably choose "Love your neighbor as yourself". This will be in print forever, so it better be a good one. Actually, in youth ministry a Scripture in First Timothy is one I use a lot with my kids. 1 Timothy 4:11, "Let no one slight you because you are young, but make yourself an example to believers in speech and behavior, in love, fidelity, and purity." Just because you are young doesn't mean you can't be a leader in your life and matters of faith. I have a passion for helping youth, and so it has always been one of my favorite scriptures.

You might even substitute the word gay in there, instead of young. I would think that would be helpful.

Yeah, I guess you could.

I know you were elected to the position of General Conference Delegate for the 2004 Conference in Pittsburgh. One of the hot issues was the discussion of changing some policies in the United Methodist Church Book of Discipline concerning gays in the church. Can you talk a little bit about that?

At first I was surprised when someone asked me if I would consider running for the position, but was pleased to be asked. When I was actually elected, I felt a great sense of honor to have been given that responsibility. As we got closer to the conference opening, sometimes it became less of an honor. It was a struggle at times, getting tons of mail on numerous issues. One of the main issues, of course, was homosexuality and how the church was dealing with that. In looking back at the mail, I'd guess that eighty percent of the letters said that we should not have gays in the church, especially in pastoral positions and twenty percent who said gays in general should be supported. That's when I began feeling a little overwhelmed. I then went to some of my friends for support.

I don't know how much of the story you want, but an e-mail was sent out that pretty much "outed" me to the whole delegation. I got a call from a friend asking me if I knew it had gone out.

How did you feel, knowing that the word was out?

Well, my life is an open book. I just don't read it to everybody. It was actually a positive e-mail. It was someone who was saying that they had known me for a long time and wanted the others to know that being gay would not keep me from doing a good job as a delegate. I just felt a little laid open, somehow. It was done in a loving way but still left things open for problems.

I talked to a couple of friends to get their opinions on what to do. They suggested getting everything out in the open. I came back to the office and called a staff meeting to let them know what was going on, and if they had questions about my being gay or anything else to come talk to me. I got complete support and affirmation. It turned out to be a helpful incident to send me off to conference.

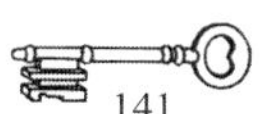

Wasn't there a letter sent to the Bishop and Cabinet questioning your sexual orientation when you first came to this position as conference youth director?

Yes, and the Bishop and Cabinet didn't ask me if it was true or not true. They just said I was the one they wanted for this job, end of story. I appreciated their looking at me as a whole person, and how my gifts and graces could be used to help youth. We need to look at the whole person. That applies to everyone.

Were there any repercussions when you got to General Conference?

No, I did the same thing with the other delegates that I had done at my office and, even though we weren't all on the same page with the issues, we agreed to treat each other with respect as part of the same delegation.

I remember calling you during the first week of General Conference and you were having a great time. Remind me of your comments.

That first week, we were breaking up into small groups, and there were United Methodists from all over the world dialoguing since my sub-group was global missions.

There were people from Bulgaria, Russia, and Africa. All of these cultures and different languages really made me aware of the global church. We, in America, just don't have any concept of the big picture. These people are dealing with severe starvation and poverty and the HIV crisis. It was a big wake-up call to me as to how many other things we could be dealing with other than who a person loves.

Tell me about the second week, when the homosexuality and the Book of Discipline were being discussed.

The second week got a lot more interesting and more difficult. One of the hardest things was not letting on how much I was hurting through the proceedings, so I held a lot of stuff in. I didn't want them to know that what was being said from the floor was hurtful. "If you're gay you can't serve the church as a pastor," and all the discussion on gay marriage--it was crazy! On the issue of teen suicide--people wouldn't even consider some kind of network to try to prevent it. Issue after issue kept piling up. It was very hurtful to have people celebrate excluding you from the church.

How did you get through all of that?

Fortunately, I found a group of friends, like-spirits and gay pastors who would meet in the evenings to commiserate and support each other. That was very helpful. I also had friends from home calling me and asking how I was doing.

Did you think about who Jesus was during these proceedings?

I thought a lot about who Jesus wasn't! That concept played out in some of the conversations going on around me. From what I understood, people were a lot more respectful of each other this time than they were four years ago. The side conversations were about winning the vote and not letting "them" win.

The thing that was hard was that the language didn't improve in the Discipline, but it got even narrower and more limiting. Pastors not only were forbidden to do marriages or unions, but they couldn't even celebrate anniversaries with same-sex couples. That was the worst day at General Conference.

Did you ever feel like just throwing in the towel and leaving the church?

I don't know that I ever felt like leaving the Church, but I do keep asking why the Church doesn't understand. How can my understanding of who Christ is, and what he came to teach us be so different from someone else's understanding of who Christ is? Why can't we even have a discussion? The opposition wouldn't even allow the conversation to take place. I would like the opportunity to witness, as a Christian, how Christ's love has manifested in my life.

I know you had an amazing experience on Tuesday evening after the sessions were over. Tell me about that.

It had been an awful day at the conference. The proceedings were hard, and we'd been in session from eight-thirty in the morning until eleven o'clock at night. After it was over, I felt like I needed some time to just walk and think. I got lost and ended up in downtown Pittsburgh in an area that I really should not have been in at that time of night. As I was walking, a gentleman sort of turned a corner behind me and he called out to me to stop. Of course, at that moment, my heart was up in my throat. I knew I couldn't outrun him, so I just decided to see what happened. He called out again and asked me to stop for a second.

When I stopped, he walked up to me and started talking. I was waiting for him to ask for money for drugs, and I was ready to give him my money and get out of there. But instead, he started to explain why he had singled me out.

He said that when he saw me walking down the street, he hoped I would talk to him. He said that he looked at me and knew that I was a holy man. That really sort of took me back, because I didn't have any buttons or ID that would indicate that, or that I was even involved with a church. We probably talked for close to an hour. He told me that he had just gotten out of prison the week before, and that he was living in a shelter. He had started that evening to go out and try to find some drugs, which is what he'd been in trouble for before. But he said that when he saw me and felt that I was holy, he wanted to talk instead. It just blew me away. It's amazing whom God will put in your life when you are struggling. This homeless man on the street just appeared, and I knew he was serving a purpose somehow. I knew it was a holy time for me, too.

As it got later and later, the man asked me where I was staying. When I told him how far away it was, he insisted on walking me back to my hotel. He said I wasn't safe alone.

When we finally got back to the hotel, he asked me if I would pray with him for just a minute. I guess the part I forgot to mention is that he had told me his name was Steven, but for some reason I kept calling him James. When I began to pray for him, I almost called him James again but corrected myself. When I ended with an "amen," I figured we were finished, but he started praying for me. Being the crier that I am, I began to weep. He thanked God for me and for my support in keeping him from doing drugs that night. He gave me a hug and was gone.

That whole experience really brought back to me the fact that no one can take God away from me--not the Church--not any person could take away God's call in my life.

When I got back to my room, I kept thinking about why the name James kept coming up so I looked up the book of James in the Bible. This is what it said:

"My brothers, whenever you have to face trials of many kinds, count yourselves supremely happy, in the knowledge that such testing of your faith breeds fortitude, and if you give fortitude full play you will go on to complete a balanced character and will fall short of nothing."

Brian, you may have just found your Scripture--at least for a little while.

Bruce and Virginia

Civil Rights-Always

I first knew of Bruce when I read his book Can Homophobia Be Cured? *The tongue-in-cheek title caught my eye initially, but the helpful information and compassionate approach kept me interested in its contents from start to finish. I was glad I'd added it to my library. I never dreamed I'd have the opportunity to meet and work with Bruce and his wife Virginia in the future.*

I was in Dallas at a Jurisdictional Meeting of the Parents Reconciling Network in 2005 when I heard their names mentioned as reconciling parents and committee members, and a light bulb went off. They weren't able to come to this particular meeting, but I knew I would eventually meet them.

We met in the fall of 2005 at the Reconciling Ministries Network Convocation at Lake Junaluska over Labor Day weekend during the parents' pre-convocation get- together. They were delightful people and full of enthusiasm for the work to be done in educating, supporting and advocating in the area of homosexuality and the Church. After getting better acquainted with Bruce and Virginia, I knew they would have much to contribute to Voices From the Kingdom, *so we set up an interview time. I wasn't disappointed.*

Could you share your backgrounds. Were you United Methodist or something else?

Virginia: Actually, we were both members of the Church of the United Brethren in Christ, a denomination started in the early 1800's by Phillip William Otterbein and originated in the Pennsylvania-Maryland area. We followed Methodist policies. There was a very small membership in Wisconsin, where we both grew up--our younger years. Our fathers were both pastors in that denomination. There were only twenty-nine churches in the conference. It was very much a family. It was very pietist--in a good sense--seeing justice as a part of our ministry, much like the Church of the Brethren. As a result, I grew up always understanding that we were to serve Christ in whichever way Christ led. I grew up in a parsonage. My father was a chaplain in the army during the Second World War, so we were moved around a lot. After the war was over he became the pastor of the church in Santa Cruz, New Mexico, and a Bible teacher at McCurdy School, which is now a United Methodist Mission School. I'm a graduate of McCurdy School. Then I went to Indiana Central College, now the University of Indianapolis--our denominational school.

Let's review some history here in connection with the United Brethren and the Methodist denominations. Didn't they merge into what we now know as the United Methodist denomination?

Bruce: The 1945 merger between the United Brethren and the Evangelical Church made up the United Evangelical Brethren and that's the church that merged with the Methodist Church to make the United Methodist Church. In other words, we've been through two mergers. The UB and the Evangelical to make the Evangelical Brethren, and then that church merged with the various Methodist Churches in 1967 forming your United Methodist Church.

Bruce, you grew up as a "preacher's kid," just like Virginia.

B: Yes, our fathers were good friends, and we knew each other at church camp when we were six or seven years old.

I know that you both ended up answering calls to the ministry, just like your fathers. Share those experiences.

B: That's a long story. When it was time for college at Indiana Central College, I came from Minnesota and she came from New Mexico. We connected, and before we really realized who each other was we'd had a date. We both graduated from Indiana Central College--Virginia as a nurse. She wanted to be a doctor, but her professor of biology wouldn't recommend a woman for medical school, so Virginia became a nurse in a program at Indiana Central connected with a Methodist Hospital in Indianapolis.

How long after that did you feel called to the ministry?

V: My call to ministry came much later. I always wanted to be in Christian service from the age of fifteen at summer camp when I dedicated my life to Christ, so that was always in my background. My dream was to be a medical missionary. I worked at hospitals until our first child was born, and then I was a full-time mom for quite a long time.

We eventually became civil rights workers in Mississippi--Greenville, Mississippi--with the Delta Ministry from 1965 to 1967. I worked there with that organization in voter rights and health care teaching--things like that, among plantation workers. My call to ministry didn't come until 1974. It was a very clear call. I was forty-four, so it was a second career call but I really felt like I was coming home when I went to seminary. This is what I wanted to do all along, but was avoiding it.

Where did you go to seminary?

V: I went two years to Drew Theological Seminary in New Jersey, and then finished two years at Pacific School of Religion in Berkley with an MDiv and a Masters in pastoral counseling.

Bruce, were you already a pastor at this time?

B: I was never a pastor. I'm a clergyman, but never had a church. My calling has always been to what the United Methodist calls an appointment beyond the local church. First of all, before I graduated seminary I had had almost ten years experience as a newspaper man. When I graduated seminary, I was asked to fill in as youth editor for the EUB Church because their editor had died, and it was a long time until General Conference. I spent eleven years in Dayton, Ohio, editing the publications--the story papers and church curriculum that the kids read.

Then in '65, things were heating up in civil rights. Both of us had been involved in different ways in civil rights activities in Dayton. I got a call one day, asking us to come to Mississippi with the Delta Ministry, which was a civil rights organization sponsored by the National Council of Churches. We were down there for a little over two years, at the height of the tension in the Civil Rights Movement in '65 and '67. Virginia served as a nurse and also as a teacher in one of the freedom schools. We were working with impoverished sharecroppers, especially those who had been thrown off the plantations for registering to vote.

Did you have all of your children by this time?

V: Our youngest was three months old when we went to Mississippi. We took the whole family, which was not what most civil rights workers did because of

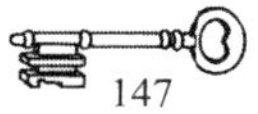

the danger. The youngest was three months old, and the oldest was ten. We'd take our four little boys to church--to white churches on Sunday--all dressed up, and on Monday inevitably the pastor would ask us not to come back. These were Methodist and Presbyterian churches.

Was that because they found out you were involved in the civil rights movement?

V: Yes.

Were there black churches you could attend?

V: Yes, we finally did. We felt welcome in the black churches. I did some home schooling with our kids, as far as Sunday school was concerned. We had our Sunday school at home. They went through the public school system. That whole experience pretty much shaped all of our lives. We used to joke that everything we learned about justice we learned in Mississippi.

B: That experience had a lot to do with how we felt later on when we were dealing with LGBT people.

Would this be a good time to talk about your finding out that you have a son who is gay and what your past experience with justice issues contributed to making that adjustment in your family life?

B: I just want to say that having had the experience of not being welcome in churches, we knew a little bit what that might be like. We understood our GLBT friends who had been told they weren't welcome at different churches. Virginia, do you want to continue?

V: I had graduated from seminary and was in the ordination process, and was an associate pastor of a church in El Sobrante, California. Our second son, Phil, came out to me. He did this because he and a lesbian friend were going to have a class on human sexuality and were going to come out to the church they were attending, Trinity United Methodist in Berkley, which is now a Reconciling United Methodist Church. As a part of that class, they would be talking about what it meant to be a gay man or a lesbian in the Church. He wanted to make sure it was all right with me, because he was concerned about my process of ordination--that it would limit that or cause me problems in the process. I assured him that it wouldn't. I cried because I was concerned about his safety. He was the only one of our sons who really wanted to go on to pastoral ministry. From the time he was in confirmation class he felt called to the ministry. He dropped out of college after two and a half years of pre-ministry classes. Although the atmosphere of the college where he was going was pretty progressive it was still homophobic, so he had an uncomfortable time there.

B: He dropped out of school partly because he knew by then that he could never be ordained as an out, gay man--in our denomination.

What were your initial reactions upon hearing your son say that he was gay?

V: I had suspected for a long time that Phil was gay, so it was confirming what I felt I already knew, but I needed him to confirm it. Bruce had a different reaction.

B: Yes, what we said to Phil, of course, was as loving as possible, but in my own heart I felt that this was maybe just a phase. One thing I wondered was, did this happen just because we'd moved to San Francisco? I was really dumb about homosexuality and I was homophobic. However, it took me only a couple of weeks of studying and talking to Phil and others to realize how far off base I was. In a sense, I consider myself a "recovering homophobe." I think that in our society straights never fully overcome our homophobia. Even some gay and lesbian people have trouble overcoming it.

I have read your book *Can Homophobia be Cured* and found it to be very helpful. How long did it take you to write it after you found out Phil was gay?

V: It was actually fourteen years later.

B: Phil came out in 1974 and the book was published in 1994.

V: I'm sure parents who were dealing with the issue then realize how little was written in 1974. Virginia Mellencott's *Is the Homosexual My Neighbor?, The Pink Triangle*, and maybe a couple of others, but that was about it.

V: One thing that I might bring up here is what my senior pastor's reaction was when I told him Phil was gay. When Phil told me, I was heading out for our church retreat which I was leading. I sat down at a spare moment with the senior pastor and I told him that Phil was gay. He physically edged two feet away from me. I mean he really had trouble with that. He said, "Just don't talk about it." That was also his reaction at the church, but I did talk about it.

The significant turning point for us was the 1980 General Conference. Phil went with us, and we went with Affirmation, the gay and lesbian caucus. Affirmation was staying in a kind of a sleazy, pay-by-the-hour motel. That was the only place they could find in Indianapolis. It was really a marvelous

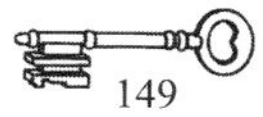

experience for us because Affirmation people just took us in. They knew we were ignorant and they helped us, and we were part of the witness every day at the General Conference. In the evening we would all have a time together to debrief and sing. For me it was a spiritual experience. That was a time of really feeling supported, particularly by Affirmation.

I know you have been instrumental in starting the Parents Reconciling Network. How does this all fit into a timeline with the publication of Bruce's book and other work you two have done?

B: We started talking about a parents' group in 2000. For three or four years it was mostly just talk. We talked to a lot of people who might be interested and we were encouraged by our conversations, but nobody wanted to bite the bullet and get it going.

V: It was really at the 1996 General Conference that we realized we needed more witnesses. We needed the parents there. We talked with Mark Bowman, and he was really enthusiastic--but again, it took us four years to get rolling.

B: Just to get the timeline right, from '92 to '96 I was on the denominational twenty-seven member Committee to Study Homosexuality. We met four times a year--four days at a time for four years to produce the report for the United Methodist Church. The General Conference almost voted to accept, but it didn't end up passing. That had a lot to do with my approach to things. Phillip's coming out and this experience with the committee turned the justice issue of homosexuality from just an "issue" to a real-life question that we had to deal with. It took a while for it to "cook." So, in 2000, Virginia and I started talking about what we might do. Leading up to the 2000 General Conference in Cleveland, we mailed out about 250 letters to parents from a list given to us by the Reconciling Ministries people. We asked them to be there with us. We designed big 4" by 6" badges saying, "Our Child is of Sacred Worth." Those badges were designed to be seen all the way across the convention hall. Virginia had a sign made that we could hang from a table: "Parents Reconciling Network" and we had 200 buttons made. This was all just Ginny and me, at this stage.

At the semi-annual Reconciling Ministries Convocation down in Denton, Texas, we had a session just for parents, and out of that I was asked to report to the larger general group. I told them that at the General Conference, "We're going to have a hundred parents." I had no assurance at all that we would, but it sounded like a good idea. We had made 200 badges, however, and by the time the General Conference was over, 120 people had come to our table and asked for badges. It was really inspiring.

Bruce, did you write *Can Homophobia Be Cured*? in anticipation of having it available at one of the General Conferences, or how did that come about? What inspired you to do that?

B: Ironically, it was my hatred of writing. I've written all my life--I had just finished a book on medical ethics, which is my field, titled, *First Do No Harm*. I was down at Abingdon Press having lunch with my editor and she asked me what I was going to write next. I didn't want to write anything "next". So I thought of something I was sure they couldn't do. I said, "I'd like to write a book that tells the other side of the gays and lesbians, transgender and bisexuals--the side our church rarely tells," She paused a second and then said, "I think we could do that."

I was trapped. I'd had no intention of doing that, but I really wanted somebody to do it. They liked my writing, so I ended up doing it.

The title, *Can Homophobia Be Cured*? is an interesting concept. Did it come from the idea that some folks think homosexuality can and needs to be cured? Is that where the tongue-in-cheek idea came from?

B: Yes.

V: Exactly. I should say that really the "germ" of the Reconciling Parents Network began to grow at the Atlanta Convocation of Reconciling Ministries when Bruce and I led a pre-convocation seminar with parents. We contacted a few that we knew and some who were recommended. That was 1997--Bruce ended up having heart bypass surgery, so some of the other parents helped me with that seminar. There were twenty-five of us and we did a lot of talking. We didn't talk structure or organization, but we talked about the need for parents to be more active. That was after Mark Bowman had talked to us, so we kind of knew what we wanted to do, but didn't have a clue how to do it. It was just helpful to know there was support for that idea.

B: Interesting numbers--those mailings that we did brought in a disappointing thirty-five people who were willing to come to General Conference after I'd promised to have 100. The thirty-five turned into the 120 wearing the badge including a couple from other countries. We now have around 1000 on the network--a thousand parents!

V: People like John and Linda Lewis who were instrumental, or Jamie Stroud who was the first chair of the steering committee of PRN, didn't get the mailing because they weren't on any list we had, but they showed up at General

Conference, seeing the other badges and wanting one for themselves. They were the ones who were the most enthusiastic about getting involved.

How are you feeling about the direction the United Methodist Church is currently taking? Is there hope on the other side of the frustration, or are you discouraged? How do you see the future?

V: My feeling is that the Judicial Council, in their decision to stand by the pastor who refused church membership to a gay man on the grounds that he was an unrepentant sinner, aroused some of the people who have been on the fence with the question of homophobia in the Church. Most thoughtful Christians would feel revulsion about turning anyone away from being a member. I think it might be helpful in increasing the number of Reconciling Congregations, because now more than ever we need to make clear that we welcome gay people.

B: I agree completely, but I would like to put it in a longer context, as far as we personally are concerned. We've been involved in justice issues since--well, in Ginny's case--since the seventh grade. She was suspended from school for refusing to sing in the seventh grade graduation choir because they weren't going to let the two black kids in the school sing in the choir. She refused to sing and was suspended. There's an early justice issue. We've been--throughout our lives because of our parents' example--been involved in justice issues. When this came home to us, it became more real to us but it wasn't brand new. For example, racism--we worked in the fifties for Ohio fair housing. Virginia was actually named Woman of the Year in Dayton, because of her work to combat racism in housing. We lived for ten years in a neighborhood that became largely African American, and we were quite satisfied there until we got the call to go to Mississippi. That was two more years of working on racism, and at the same time we were working on sexism. As time went on and the different issues raised themselves, we became involved. We consider ourselves not one-issue people, but people who learned at our parents' knees that Jesus came to show love. I remember asking my dad, one time, "Why did Jesus come?" I was nine years old. I can remember it quite vividly. My dad said, "Jesus came to show us what God is like." I think that's kind of a background for our wanting to help the oppressed, the poor, and the excluded--to make the Church what we think Jesus intended the Church to be.

It sounds like you two are in this for the long haul, even if the Church comes to change kicking and screaming.

B: Yes. We've been to all but one General Conference since 1980, lobbying each time for change in the Discipline from the restrictive words. We've been involved in Affirmation. Virginia was in on the founding of the Reconciling Ministries. She might want to say something about that.

V: Yes, I do. In 1982 I was chosen to be the only straight member of the Affirmation Steering Committee--recommended by a lesbian friend. It was while I was on the steering committee that they came up with this crazy idea to organize congregations to become Reconciling Congregations. In a Denver Affirmation Steering Committee meeting they presented two wonderful plans. One was for organizing the churches into a kind of grass roots organization, and the other was to plan for a magazine or newsletter. I was on the committee that talked about the newsletter. The idea was to have a mimeographed newsletter that could be mailed out to people once a month. We had a short mailing list, as Affirmation was a relatively small organization, but powerful people. We had a man who had been editor of *Motive*, B.J.Stiles, who protested and said, "No! We need to make this the best quality magazine we can possibly do, to show the Church we take it seriously." That was the birth of what became *Open Hands*. It was exciting to be in on that. It was for gays and lesbians and their supporters. I was really disappointed when they couldn't afford to put it out any more. It was a powerful witness. It was sponsored by the Reconciling Ministries program.

Are there particular scriptures that are helpful to you in your work or just in life in general--especially when the going gets rough?

B: Everybody is selective about what they choose out of the Bible to guide their lives. There are those who see the Bible as a harsh, judgmental book. We have friends and relatives who are that way. I would say that rather than pick out a particular proof text, I would look for Jesus' basic message. To the Sermon on the Mount, for example--Blessed are the meek. Blessed are the peacemakers. That's the real Jesus. Throughout the New Testament and in parts of the Hebrew Scriptures, there are interesting insights. "What does the Lord require of thee, but to do justice, love kindness, and walk humbly with your God?" If I had to center on one, that would be the one that I'd pick.

V: One of the most authentic that I believe we need to carry with us always is to "Love God with all your heart and mind and soul, and love your neighbor as yourself. On this lies all the law and the commandments." I think Jesus said it very clearly.

Do you have any closing thoughts that you want to finish up with? Anything we didn't say that you would like to talk about now?

B: Yes, I have something that needs to be said. We talked about founding the Parents Reconciling Network, and we certainly did, but there was what I call a second founding--in that we got it going, but it needed a good committee to carry it on. Those folks just turned up and organized a really good committee. We had a period of sickness when we couldn't be involved, and they took the ball and ran with it. They turned it into a wonderful network. I want to be sure it doesn't sound like we were the only ones.

V: There are times we have given up on the Church or I should say we wanted to--we became pretty discouraged, but our feeling throughout all of our lives has been that the Church is our home, in a way. It's where we need to be, so any talk about leaving the Church would just be almost unthinkable. It's been our whole life. We still hold onto the feeling that we can be a voice for change in the Church. Our organizations, the movement, will eventually change the Church--that is eventually going to happen.

Whether the conservatives want it or not, it's going to happen. I think it's going to happen sooner than we realize.

Doug and Chris

A Place to Call Home

I had known Doug's family's name from hearing it in the community, but did not know them personally. For some reason, I knew that the family had a son who was gay. So, in the winter of 2002 when I heard that Doug and a friend named Chris were coming to perform for a concert series given by Doug's home church, my husband and I decided to go. It was one of the most beautiful, inspirational and spiritual hours of music we had ever experienced. Doug's tenor voice was so clear and warm. It was obvious when Chris played the piano that he had a relationship with the instrument as well as the music.

After the concert, we met the two young performers, who by now we had confirmed as partners through the write-up in the program. I gave them a copy of Cleaning Closets, *and we purchased their CD, "Imago Dei."*

Three years later, we heard that Doug and Chris were to be back in town for another concert. We immediately put it on our calendar and gave away the basketball tickets we had for that same afternoon.

It dawned on me that Doug and Chris might have some insights to offer about their spirituality through music and their experiences in attending an open and welcoming United Methodist Church in Indianapolis, so I called them. They were quite willing to share their individual faith stories and their personal story as partners of fourteen years. Both men shared with me that they were forty-four years old. Doug has blonde hair, a ruddy complexion, and an easy laugh. Chris has more of an olive complexion and seemed more serious, although his smile was quite warm and engaging.

We did the interview at the church Doug attended as a youth.

Doug, tell me what it was like, growing up in the United Methodist Church in the Midwest.

Doug: My roots were here in the United Methodist Church. Most of the kids I spent time with were involved in the church--either through their family's membership or through neighborhood association or through the Boy Scout Troop the church sponsored. My life did evolve around here--prosperous youth program--got a lot of spiritual foundation--although it was probably more social. It was all about our friends at school and the youth group.

Did you hear anything about homosexuality in church?

I didn't really hear much about that in church. A couple of thoughts come to mind, though. They had a summer day camp one week, and in looking back, I now recall that I was drawn to the male counselor. I didn't know what it was, but I just remember feeling good about a genuine affection that was given back. We were probably fairly progressive for a United Methodist Church. We had a sexuality weekend where we learned about procreation and all the right sexual terms. I recall there was some mention of attraction to same sex, but it wasn't a big deal. I never felt judged here, only loved and supported.

What about you, Chris, where are your roots?

Chris: Well, I grew up Catholic. I probably knew in junior high that I was gay, but of course didn't talk about it. I would visit other churches to play the piano every once in awhile. I don't have very fond memories of having to sit through sermons about the evils of homosexuality. Being there and not being able to say anything, I just internalized a lot of negative things. I've always played in churches, some Catholic, some Methodist, and I've always struggled with not feeling comfortable until I started playing at our church, Broadway United Methodist.

Were these churches fundamentalist churches?

C: No, they were like Presbyterian, Christian.

Let's talk a little about your relationship with each other.

C: We've been together--it'll be fourteen years in June. I think our connection with Broadway and the United Methodist Church, and just church in general, has helped our relationship. Our music is a way for us to express our faith. There are so many things I disagree with in the Church. I don't know, I guess I just take what's okay with me, and leave the rest. Spirituality and church give me a solid foundation, a sense of purpose that supports and encourages our relationship with each other.

Did you meet at church?

C: No, we met through the Indianapolis Men's Chorus, a gay men's chorus. They practiced at the Broadway Church, and so we met there and eventually started going there.

D: It's difficult to separate the faith and spirituality from the music. It's been an amazing and healthy conduit for us to express ourselves. It's also been a tool for me to explore my faith. The text of music has allowed me to grow spiritually and develop my own sense of God and spirituality. The music that most speaks to my faith journey has simple references to love, acceptance, and inclusiveness.

I have certainly heard you express your faith when I've attended your performances. Has anyone ever put two and two together when you've performed, or has it not come up?

D: We don't perform outside church very often. Our schedules don't allow us to.

C: Most churches where we've sung are like this church in Salina--accepting of us. We did perform at an MCC in Indianapolis, as well as our own church, Broadway United Methodist. I think it was safe for them to say that we're together. They did introduce us as a couple at MCC.

D: I think we're both out--I wouldn't say we're activists. At our age, being blessed to be in a big city and spending fourteen years together and building a community around that, I don't feel like I have to hide it, nor will I. On the other hand, my life is my life, so look at me by my character and how I produce and interact with people. What I do in my bedroom isn't anybody's business.

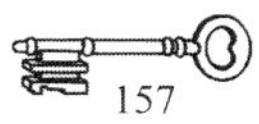

What about your professional lives--are they in music or something else?

C: I just work part time as an organist at my church. I used to do some accounting work, but I gave that up because of the stress. I returned to school at IU to finish a music degree I never finished, so I'm in school.

D: I do some music, semi-professionally. I do some studio work, but my primary source of income is from residential real estate. I left sixteen years of non-profit fund raising and organizational management a couple of years ago to get out of the rat race and work for myself.

Tell me a little bit about your congregation in Indianapolis. How did you get started there?

C: I guess ever since the men's chorus, I've been aware of Broadway because we rehearsed there. I had always dreamed of being able to play there, because it had been around forever. It's this large Gothic building with an interesting history. The building was built in 1927. It's a wonderful place to worship. At one time it was a national pulpit. It's a downtown, urban church, so the church has struggled with keeping membership. There was a core group of older members who kept the church alive, and I don't really know how it became a safe place for gay people. The older members have been great to get to know. I thank them that they stuck it out and kept the church going. I also thank them for being accepting of us. One thing I like about Broadway is that it's not a gay church. There are older members, traditional families with children, gay families with and without children. We are at a point where it's a non-issue. Gay is not talked about every week, but other members know we are a couple and support us emotionally. They treat us like a "traditional" couple.

D: I think Phil Emerson is a name that some people will know. He really started opening things up. Another was Dick Armstrong. He was the pastor in the '70s, very liberal and pretty progressive in his thinking and theology, which allowed for a few people to feel like they could be there. I mean, years before we got there, there were transgender people attending. Things began to happen when the men's chorus started rehearsing there. Naturally, a couple of men started singing in the church choir. I remember that soon after I started attending and worshiping there I sang--I was invited to sing, and that was helpful for me to feel a part of the congregation. I recall that the warm response to my singing was a welcome surprise--it really helped me to feel genuinely accepted and included. It also came at a pivotal time in my coming-out process and helped me to accept myself and my sexuality. One of the most difficult obstacles to my coming out was reconciling my sexuality with the church. The loving acceptance I felt from the members there was so refreshing.

At one time, there was an effort to make it a Reconciling Congregation. There was a Reconciling Congregations Task Force. People from Chicago came down to help us. We struggled with that an awful lot, decided then, and still pretty much maintain today, that for whatever reason, we don't want the label. I think we feel like there's strength in not having to put the label on it. We are a reconciling congregation just by who we are, and just by the nature of our make-up. Probably sixty-plus percent of the congregation is gay. Many are couples with adopted children or children of their own. There are probably seven or eight Guatemalans--probably as many little Asian girls, and they're all growing up together. Families get together once a month in the community room. The kids play and the parents do what parents do. It's really a wonderful, wonderful place.

C: The people are great--the elderly people are there, and young families--it's nice that it's not just a gay church.

D: It takes the right kind of pastoral leadership. For a while we transitioned to the wrong pastoral leadership, for about two years, opposite of what we needed.

C: You were talking about how the Church didn't feel like it had to have a label. That kind of corresponds to how I feel about Broadway. My being gay is really a non-issue. I'm just another member taking my journey.

Do you have Scriptures that are guiding forces in your lives?

D: I would just go to 1 Corinthians 13. It's not just for weddings, but talks about what love is all about, being kind and patient, not arrogant or rude. It fits how we should treat everyone.

C: Then there's the one in Micah, about what God requires of you--to do justice, to love mercy, and to walk humbly with your God.

Since you are musicians, I should ask you what your favorite hymns or performance pieces are. Explain why they are meaningful to you.

D: I guess the first thing that comes to mind is the old altar-call, "Just As I

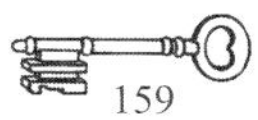

Am." To me, it says a great deal about acceptance and love. It reinforces that God accepts us just as we are.

C: I have so many that I like. I especially appreciate the traditional hymns--those written by Martin Luther, Charles and John Wesley and those that came from the Lutheran Church and the Church of England. The texts of these hymns are great poems that help me in my spiritual growth. I am not a strong supporter of the new "praise" songs that make you feel good at the moment. My strength comes from texts that give me direction, hope, and perseverance.

Let's change from Scripture and music to United Methodist Church policies. Have you tried to keep up with the broader church on the policies that are set forth in the Discipline?

D: I get frustrated and have sometimes entertained the idea of actively protesting that. If you are going to belong to an institution whose principles you don't agree with, then you either put up with it or speak out against it. Then I realized that I really don't care about the institution. The institution does not affect my life terribly, right now. We're in a community of faith, a community of people journeying together. There are people who love us the way we are, and whom we love the way they are, and that is enough for me, and it happens to be United Methodist. For me, it works--it could be MCC, it could be Hindu, it could be Jewish. I have the good fortune to sing High Holy Days for one of the synagogues in the Jewish community. It's been an eye-opener, you know--Old Testament stuff. But the thing is, it's the same story--it's love. It's all about getting along and supporting each other, being human to each other. So, we follow the struggles of the United Methodist Church by reading national magazines and we get frustrated. It just seems so unnecessary.

I just thought of a story relating to my faith journey here in this church. A very impactful youth minister, Steve Fink--he really got it, I think. He greatly influenced me as a junior high age kid through MYF and stuff. Then he went away. I heard he went to join UNICEF. I think he went to join MCC, but the story here was that he was in New York working for UNICEF. I didn't think another thing about it. As it happened, my career took me into a national fraternity headquarters, and many of the national board members are gay. I was coming out at that time. They flew me to New York for the 1985 Gay Pride Parade. My eyes were just--well, I'm seeing the underbelly and the fun of the gay community and it's just--wow--this kid from the sticks in Kansas. There were four hundred thousand people lining Fifth Avenue--I didn't know there were that many people in the world, let alone that many gay people. Here comes MCC marching with their contingency and here comes Steve Fink! It must have been ten, fifteen years since I last saw him in Kansas and I just yelled at him and we embraced and then my entourage joined MCC and marched all the way to the Village with them. It was a real affirmative thing for me to see someone for whom I had a great deal of respect and who made a real impact on me at a tender young age--in that place. It was a real divinely inspired meeting-- there's no doubt. Then I ran into him later that night in a restaurant. What are the chances of that happening? It was just neat. That's a story that comes out of the church of my youth.

Chris, do you put much energy into the conflicts of the wider United Methodist Church, or do you just concentrate on your day-to-day faith journeys in general?

C: There are times when I get really frustrated with that whole thing, but making a fuss just isn't part of my personality. I think, live as we can, in a spiritual way with each other and with our church family. I think eventually things will work out. I'm amazed how far things have come. When I was in junior high, realizing I was gay, I had no idea we would eventually be talking about gay marriage, and here we are. So I have hope that one day our society and church will treat us respectfully and provide us the same benefits and rights as heterosexual couples.

Since you brought the subject up, let's talk about gay marriage. Is that something you two feel would make your relationship more complete?

D: My thoughts on that are best expressed from an experience I had. It was for a heterosexual wedding I was involved in. There was a song from Sting , I think that's where the text came from, but it talks about the secret marriage vow that's never spoken. There aren't any of the cultural accoutrements that can sometimes weigh things down. It simplifies it to just the connection between the two people. It celebrates that. I'm beginning to think that's kind of where we are.

No earthly church has ever blessed our union
No state has ever granted us permission
No family bond has ever made us two
No company has ever earned commission

No debt was paid, no dowry to be gained
No treaty over border land or power
No semblance of the world outside remained
To stain the beauty of this nuptial hour

The secret marriage vow is never spoken
The secret marriage can never be broken

No flowers on the alter
No white veil in your hair
No maiden dress to alter
No Bible oath to swear

The secret marriage vow is never spoken
The secret marriage can never be broken.

C: Yeah, I think for us the most important thing is to be able to have benefits and rights as a couple. To feel safe in knowing that, no matter the circumstances, institutions and people respect the relationship that we share.

Have you done any of the legal work that has to be done to get your rights as a couple put in order?

D: Started it, but haven't completed it.

Doug, I know your family is supportive and would never give you any trouble by not treating you like a legally married couple with all those rights. How about your family, Chris?

C: No, not at all. We are extremely blessed to have immediate and extended families who accept us as a couple.

D: I worry about the state. You just never know. For example, we're going to Europe this summer. You never know what might happen there that could cause

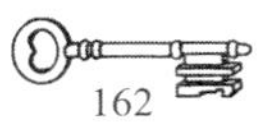

a problem. Actually, it might be better there, now that I think about it.

I guess there is a part of me that thinks there is something to say for a public celebration with friends and family.

Does the fact that you have a faith connection in your relationship influence your considering some kind of ceremony?

D: If we were to want that, we couldn't do it at our church, and I wouldn't ask our pastor to. But he would come and bless our relationship at our home.

We've talked about your families a little. Is there anything further you would like to comment on?

C: Well, I think we have both been blessed. I come from a large family with eight children, and two of us are gay. I think that has made it a little bit easier. I was just thinking, we were talking previously about the United Methodist Church and activism. There are some wonderful people in the church--clergy and others, who are publicly taking a stand--taking risks on our behalf. I just have such an appreciation for the work that they do.

D: It just occurred to me that we don't deliberately go out and seek to change things, but we do have opportunities to minister, if you want to call it that, through our music. Our current concert we are presenting is about Christmas and Jesus, but it has an acceptance tone to it. We've done PFLAG concerts for as few as 12 people, and there may be one mother sitting there struggling. If it helps her reconcile and find an acceptance, it's worth it. Maybe that's what we're here to do, and maybe that's "activism." If that's activism, then we're activists. We're just living our lives and sharing the gifts God has given us, and if that helps people, then I'm okay with that.

Do you have any other comments you'd like to make before we close?

D: Just that we're here for the long haul. We're not leaving the United Methodist Church.

Rev. Dell

In the Loopholes

Even though I had only seen Gregory Dell once, I knew he was a person I needed to include in this book. I had followed his story in the national news in 1998, when the United Methodist Judicial system brought him up on charges because he performed a commitment ceremony for a same-gendered couple after that body had forbidden it. I wanted to know what was behind his actions, and I wanted to hear it directly from him, even though some years had passed since the event had taken place.

I had met Rev. Dell briefly some years before, while I was attending a Reconciling Ministries event at a Reconciling Church three hours from where I live. He was introducing the concept of "Church Within a Church." I was curious about the idea, but was not able to go to his session because it was in conflict with another session I wanted to attend. I was still curious and still uninformed when I went to Chicago to interview him.

I was quite impressed by Rev. Dell's grasp on what he saw as problematic in the United Methodist Church and by the creative ways he had developed to deal with them. His passion and commitment to changing the attitudes and laws against those who have been marginalized by the institutional Church were evident as he choked back tears during certain parts of our interview. When I left Broadway United Methodist Church following the interview, I thought to myself, "This man gets it."

Did you grow up United Methodist or some other denomination?

Rev Dell: My family moved to a blue-collar suburb of Chicago when I was about five years old, and that was where we started attending a Methodist Church, because it was the closest church to the house--not because of any great

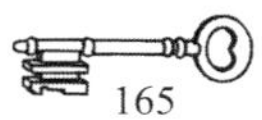

conviction or principle, but more because it was convenient. So I grew up in the Methodist Church, and of course now the United Methodist Church.

Are you from a large family?

No, two sisters, and I'm the oldest and only brother. My grandmother lived with us some of that time.

What do you remember hearing in the church you grew up in--supportive kind of preaching or condemnation?

Well, it was interesting, because the town where I grew up in Illinois was intentionally an all-white, blue-collar suburb. It was designed and operated to make sure that black people who were in the Chicago area were not moving to that village, but the church and the pastor of the Methodist Church saw issues of racial justice as core to the faith. That is to say, it wasn't an optional kind of--oh, this would be a political ramification of the faith. It was more for that church and for that pastor, in a not-always friendly environment, to say this is what our faith is about. It's really celebrating all people as God's children and as sisters and brothers. So, in terms of the Church, that was very much my experience from a very young age, through high school and college.

Did you end up having any black people in your congregation as a result of that philosophy?

Actually, what happened was that by the time I was in college, the neighboring all-black suburb had a Methodist Church and the two churches merged. The folks from St. Paul's, the black church, began to attend our church and that worked out very well. I think the foundation had been laid well, so there was this sense of just being part of what we could celebrate.

Because of this, you grew up with a principled, social justice background.

At least in terms of the commitment of the Church, it was. It wasn't, in terms of the experience, because the experience was an all-white, predominately blue-collar environment, but at least what was being proclaimed was a vision of the way in which society and the Church were called.

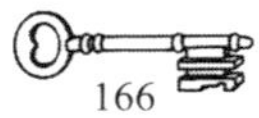

I realize there are differing opinions about our denomination's slogan "Open Hearts, Open Minds, Open Doors." What are your thoughts on that?

I think it's a travesty of hypocrisy. I think it's a cruel joke that the very same General Conference that adopted that theme reinforced and strengthened its attitude of exclusion towards some of its own sons and daughters. So I think it's offensive. It really borders on a blasphemous statement, not simply one that's morally offensive, but one that's really a slap in the face of God who created us all.

Some have said that the slogan is something we as a denomination might live into. Do you see that as a possibility?

I certainly haven't seen that. What I've seen is that the people who defended and supported the Church's majority opinion, which is an opinion of condemnation, continue to live with it as kind of a marketing tool suggesting that we are open to all people, but operating as though we are not. This is not the first time the Church has had that experience. I was reminded by an African American member of a congregation I served that when she came into a community that was racially mixed or an all-white church, they always said that everybody was welcome. Churches always say everyone is welcome, but her experience was that as a black person she could walk into that context, particularly a predominately white one, and know in a couple of minutes whether that was truly intended for her. I think lesbian, gay, bisexual persons and transgender persons, as well, have the experience that the church says it has open doors, open hearts and open minds and says all are welcome when, in fact, that's extremely conditional for the people some have found to be objectionable.

At what point in your life did you feel called to the ministry?

I think my first inclination toward parish ministry, toward pastoral ministry, was when I was in seventh or eighth grade. In fact, I got my license to preach when I was in the eighth grade, which was possible back in those early days of our history. I was also very active in the Boy Scouts, and wrestled all through high school with whether the call I felt on my life was to go into ordained ministry, or if it was to be a professional scout. I was an eagle scout by that time, as well.

Dr. King came to Chicago, and a friend of mine and I participated in a march

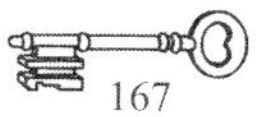

in the Berwyn community where I'd visited many times and I saw the kind of hatred and anger and disease--kind of a festering infection in our society. It had a profound affect on me. I remember saying to my friend as we were coming back, having been spit on and having rocks thrown at us, and a number of other things, I said to him, "You know, I don't think the Boy Scouts will ever be a justice organization."

That was part of the pivot for me, recognizing that the church held not only those values of connection and community that the scouts did, but that the Church was also committed, at least at the core of the Gospel, to a justice that would be inclusive of all people. That was sort of the dividing point for me when I started moving toward ordained ministry, but my real conversion to ordained ministry was when Dr. King was assassinated. I was in seminary at the time. That became the faith moment for me when I realized that this was a call, not so much to an occupation or a profession, as to a vocation.

Had you been active in other kinds of justice issues, like women's rights?

What happened was that when the so called "modern women's" movement that happened in the late sixties or really began to emerge then, we began to sort through some of what was being explored and what was being questioned and declared. It seemed to me that there were a significant number of parallels in what was being said about gender and what had been said about race. The struggles were not the same, but there were parallels, basically part of God's family being rejected because of their identity, having nothing to do with their character, their integrity, but only because of the identity God had given them. So, struggles around gender issues and sexism were a logical extension for me of my involvement in issues of racism. The same became true regarding issues of sexual orientation.

After the 1972 General Conference when the first statement was made about sexual orientation, I was chairing the Conference Board of Church and Society at the time, and there was a call for a study to be done by a task force. I hadn't thought much about sexual orientation, but as the task force began to report in on what the controversy was, I saw all the same marks again. In the same way the Bible had been used as a weapon against women and a weapon against racial inclusion. It could be used as a weapon against gay and lesbian folks. The same kind of arguments that were being made against what was really going to mess up our society and ruin our way of life were being used on sexual orientation, just as they'd been used for gender issues. So, for me again, there are significant

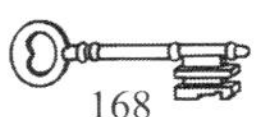

differences in the struggles around racism and sexism and heterosexism, but there are really powerful parallels, as well.

What do you think makes people hold on so tightly to the prejudices that prevent them from being inclusive?

There's not much doubt in my mind, I may be wrong, but I'm absolutely convinced it's fear and insecurity, and that the more people are uncertain about themselves and about their own value, the strength of their own integrity, the more likely they are to be afraid of something that appears to be different or someone who appears to be different. So part of the irony, I think, is that the people who are the least secure about their sexuality, in my experience, are more likely to be the least welcoming of persons whose sexuality is different from theirs.

That broadens out your job description as pastor to everyone in the Church as one who encourages people to learn to love themselves so that they will be able to love others.

Right, I think that's the pastoral side and I think it's absolutely key for all of us, lay persons and clergy alike, to minister to that fear. On the other hand, I don't think we can be naïve about that. At the same time that we understand that the motivation of the exclusionary people is a motivation that's grounded in fear and insecurity, and we need to be understanding of that and address that, we also need to realize that what is being done is injurious to people. So, while we want to be sensitive to the people who hold those views, we also have to be clear and assertive that those views need to stop injuring people the way they have. It's a two-fold approach. One is of understanding and support, the other is of insisting the damage has got to stop.

Did you start right out with your first congregation preaching social justice-- and if so, was it well received?

I've been very fortunate. My first appointment out of seminary was as an associate pastor in kind of an upper middle-class white suburb. I was working with a senior pastor who was very clear about issues of justice, economics, and racial justice, and issues around the Vietnam War which was raging at the time. He and I both preached in ways that I hope were faithful, against the war and in favor of more justice in terms of race and other issues. I think Bob caught a lot more flack than I did, he being senior pastor.

My first appointment as sole pastor was right after that, and was in a small town, a country town, kind of a conservative congregation, but it was a great five years. What I discovered is that part of where we often fail as clergy is being afraid to declare what we understand to be the "truth." If we can do that in a way that's not arrogant, not presumptuous about some kind of exclusive corner on knowing what the truth is--if we just declare it the way we see it, and we do that in a context of respect for the persons to whom we're speaking and with whom we're living, there's a possibility of going a long way.

I've been very fortunate since that first appointment, the others that followed that in Minooka, Evanston, Oak Park, and now in Chicago. The congregations have grown. There's been more enthusiasm and participation than any kind of rejection or reaction. It was actually liberating to be able to do that, not only with social justice issues, but about the way we understand the Bible, which in some ways is fundamental to these issues of justice--how we use and understand the Bible. I find that the great majority of people are excited when they find the Bible is not a science book. That the Bible was in fact written by human beings who gave us a window to the Word of God, but didn't record the words of God. Most United Methodists and most of the people who have come to the churches that I have served find that to be exciting. Some find it to be very frightening, even evil. I've been called enough names and had enough people describe me as an agent of Satan to know what that's about, but in general I think that fear has really left congregations and clergy kind of captives to an ignorance that doesn't need to be there.

Talk a little bit about Broadway United Methodist Church.

Broadway is a congregation that's been around awhile. It's over a hundred and fifteen years old. Like a lot of city churches it began with some real strength and evangelical fervor, and grew for a time. The building that originally sat on the site where we are now was constructed in the early 1900's, and had a sanctuary that would seat 400. The church never got to that size. The largest it ever grew was to about 250. It did quite well until the 'sixties, when the neighborhood began to shift--not a racial shift, but an economic shift. The crime rate went up. The profile of the community looked somewhat the same, but it was on a downhill slide.

By the time the 'eighties came, Broadway was down to about forty-five people. There was a very large stone building on this site that was an albatross, really, for the congregation to try to support and find a way to do ministry. There was a horrendous fire that burned the church to the ground. In an act of real faith those forty-five people decided to rebuild, really over the advice of the Annual Conference. When the church built a sanctuary that would seat 150, the Conference said they were even crazier than they'd been for just thinking they would continue the church.

But, as the church was literally building its new structure, it was also building its connection to the community. The pastor who was appointed during that time, the first woman pastor the church had, did a remarkable job of bringing some sense of healing and outreach to the community. So the church started to grow until that pastor was moved in 1991. That was very traumatic for the congregation, and very traumatic for that pastor. In fact, she left the pastoral ministry. The Conference really wanted to reward her for doing such a fine job, but she didn't see that as a reward. The church had a hemorrhage of membership, not an absolute one but, say from an attendance of over 100 that dropped back to about sixty.

The next pastor who came in 1991 had to deal with that dynamic, a kind of anger, I think. He retired in 1995, and recorded that the membership of the church was 260. The official statistics recorded that the average attendance on Sunday morning was 135. On my first Sunday here, which is usually a big Sunday because everybody wants to come out to find out who this new person's going to be, there were ninety people at worship. Something was going on. Someone said that was the greatest number they had seen in awhile. What we discovered was that the statistics were all wrong. The congregation had 135 members. The average attendance was closer to fifty, so we really had to start building from there. The congregation took on the challenge and excitement of creating a new understanding about what it meant to be family.

We're right at about 300 members now. Our average attendance on Sunday morning is just over 214. It's a predominately younger congregation. The average age, I think we figured, is close to thirty-five. The congregation is about equally gay and lesbian and straight in terms of sexual orientation.

This part of the city of Chicago is called "Boys' Town," historically a strong gay area. I think the enthusiasm of the people who come to worship here, both gay and straight, is because they see it as a primary commitment to celebration--not one of tolerance. In fact, every Sunday Vernice, the other pastor, and I will begin the introduction by saying that this church does not believe in tolerance. We're glad you're here, but we don't tolerate, because toleration is something you do for those you'd just as soon not be around. This church believes in

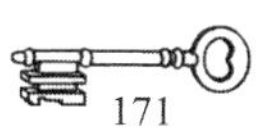

celebrating our identities, which means that because you brought the color of skin you brought today, or the gender that you brought today, or the sexual orientation that you brought today, you've enriched the experience of all of us. That's the foundational value I would say is lived out here. So, Broadway, in that sense, is doing pretty well.

What kind of ministries does the church have?

First of all, there's a heavy focus on worship, because worship is seen not as just an activity for the gathered community, a nurturing activity--it's also seen as an evangelistic outreach. We have a lot of visitors every Sunday. There are a number of people who testify that Broadway worship literally saved their lives. They were convinced that the Christian message had only one focus, and that was one of rejection or of closed-mindedness of the people who are straight. Part of our outreach is that we are very intentional about treating each worship service as a vehicle that in some primary way is a vehicle for people who are just walking in the door for the first time, some of them scared to death. So, we are very intentional about saying that our worship service is part of our outreach.

This is also a neighborhood and part of the city where there are a lot of homeless youth. It's kind of a magnet nationally for run-away and cast-away teenagers. Runaways, I think, are obvious to folks, but castaways are the gay and lesbian kids whose families have thrown them out. They come to this neighborhood, and as homeless kids they are particularly vulnerable to the drugs and prostitution, the crime. There's a minimum amount of services for them.

We've been working strongly--in fact I have a meeting today with one of the community organizers who's been working on police abuse and harassment of kids. We're involved in homeless youth, both in terms of the services that are provided to them through a number of agencies that we're part of, and also with our relationship with the police. We're trying to develop training models and accountability models for officers. There's a homeless shelter in the area that we're involved with. There are a lot of volunteer opportunities throughout the year.

I'd say a major part of our involvement is social action witness, ranging from sexual orientation issues to the war in Iraq. Our focus on racism is an ongoing focus, because that's still a dynamic that we struggle with in our congregation and in our area. Chicago is still the most segregated city in the country. We're fortunate to have more diversity in this area than in most parts of Chicago. That's a big part of our ministry.

Sometime, probably not too long after you came to this congregation, the news was full of the reporting of a commitment ceremony you performed for two men in your congregation--an act that resulted in your being brought up on charges. Take us through that experience and the results of the trial that took place.

I've been doing services for gay and lesbian couples since 1982. The first one was in Evanston. I've done over thirty services. In 1996, the General Conference passed the statement in the Social Principles that those services were not to be done. Jimmy Creech, a good friend and former classmate, did a service and was brought to trial. He was exonerated in the trial, because his defense was that the Social Principles were not binding. They say they're not binding. They're stated in the "best of the prophetic tradition for the persuasion and guidance of the Church." Jimmy's trial ended with a verdict of not guilty. Then a group of bishops asked for a declaratory decision from the Judicial Council. That declaratory decision was laid down in the summer of 1998. I'd been here three years, had been doing services all along and had another one planned. In the summer of 1998, the Judicial Council said that that one Social Principle, only that one and certainly not the ones dealing with race or gender, but that one was binding for the church. That put clergy under a mandate not to do those services.

I went ahead with the service I'd been planning. That attracted some publicity, not of our own planning. It was not intended to be some kind of a witness. I had actually counseled that summer with clergy determining that I didn't think it was a good time to do an act of public witness--that we needed to shape our strategy differently to make a difference at the General Conference in the year 2000.

Nevertheless, this one attracted attention and resulted in a complaint, and eventually a trial with a lot of publicity. I was charged with disobedience to the Order and Discipline of the United Methodist Church--the same charge they made against Jimmy. My defense was that I intentionally broke the rule, knowing that the rule was binding, but that my ordination called me to be in ministry to all people. The Denomination and certainly the Annual Conference and bishops were aware that this congregation at that time was about thirty-five per cent gay and lesbian.

Basically, what the Church said to me was that I had an ordination vow and needed to be in ministry to all people. I tried to do that--to baptize, to confirm, to teach, to preach, to bury, to visit, and to celebrate those very special covenants of commitment and love. There wasn't any way I could practice that ministry to everyone else and then to tell one group of people in the congregation, "This ministry is not available to you." So, my defense was that it was the result of wanting to be obedient to the Order and Discipline and the Church that I broke the rule. We thought it was a great defense. It didn't work, but it sounded good on paper.

The trial court found me guilty of disobedience, and then the penalty phase was an indefinite suspension. The way they stated the penalty was that I was suspended until I recanted in writing, repudiating what I'd done, and that I would pledge not to do a service again, or if the rule changed, the suspension would end. Of course I refused to make that statement, but we appealed basically on the merit of the case, and the appeals committee denied our appeal, but said that there was an error of Church law which states that you can't be suspended indefinitely--there has to be a time limit.

The appeals committee said that I would be suspended until either those first conditions were met or until one year had passed. At the end of the year the suspension was over. For that year, from the appointment year of 1999 to 2000, I was prohibited from pastoral ministry and served as director of In All Things Charity for that year. That freed me up to work full time on lobbying for the 2004 General Conference.

The concept of Church Within a Church came from this congregation. Could you explain what that means?

It was a direct result of the 2000 General Conference. When we went to the Conference, In All Things Charity, which was the movement that I was executive director for, had become an agent for a coalition of progressive groups in the Church on issues of sexual orientation. MFSA, Affirmation, Reconciling Congregations Program, United Methodists of Color for a Fully Inclusive Church, we were a working coalition.

We spent a lot of time working toward the 2000 General Conference, and one of the things we said was that we had been strong on the analysis of theology and argument, but we'd been weak in sharing stories. Our strategy leading up through 1999 was to have people share their stories in personal letters to the delegates to the General Conference, to be sure that the humanity of the people whom the legislation was most directly affecting was going to be made apparent to that General Conference in a way we had not done before in all the years we'd been working on the issue.

I think, frankly, we were successful in doing this. Every delegate to General Conference received at least five letters from lay people and clergy persons who shared their stories. We did not abandon the issue of argument in terms

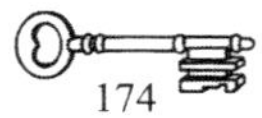

of what we are called to be as people of Christ, but we wanted to join this together with that human side. It was a powerful experience when we got to General Conference.

There was one incident that took place that convinced me that we needed to begin opening a different avenue than we'd pursued before, and that was in the Faith and Order Legislative Committee at General Conference which had responsibility for all the legislation on sexual orientation. A young man in that legislative section stood up and gave his testimony of being an active lay person in the United Methodist Church since he was a child, of being in a multiracial family, of having given his gifts and received gifts from the Church, but that he was gay. Now, the Church was basically saying that he was not good, that there was something essentially wrong with him for being gay and wanting to express his love in faithful ways. It was a very powerful moment.

There were several moments of silence after he spoke. Then a delegate stood up in tears and said, " I came here absolutely convinced that there should be no change in the position on homosexuality, that we needed to tighten things even more. What I have heard today has changed my life forever." It was a very powerful moment. Ten minutes later she voted to strengthen the restrictions.

That, to me, is the testimony of the 2000 General Conference. Good hearted people who can be moved and were moved by personal stories, as well as by argument, were so frightened that they could not do what God called them to do. At the end of that General Conference, I sent out a letter to all of those who had been part of the coalition suggesting that perhaps it was time to start thinking about a model that would be correspond to that of the Professing Church in Germany during the rise of the Nazis. That was a group of persons who insisted they were still the Church, but could no longer cooperate with the official Church that had become part of Hitler's agenda. It was out of that conversation, out of that letter, and then out of the Reconciling Ministries Convocation for which I was doing a workshop, in which I began to formulate Church Within a Church.

Church Within a Church is very intentional about saying as a movement, we're no longer going to spend our efforts trying to reform the United Methodist Church. We will support those who do and some of us individually will do that. We are not committed to remaining in the Church. We are not committed to leaving the church. We are committed to be the Church of a fully inclusive welcome. We are planting Church Within a Church congregations. The first one we planted in California is the "Bloom in the Desert Ministries," and they began by developing a congregation in the Methodist spirit of progressive and liberal Christianity. They have a worshiping congregation of about forty-five. They have affiliated with the United Church of Christ as well as keeping their Methodist affiliations, but they are not a United Methodist congregation. We are not planting United Methodist Churches, because if we do we're planning churches that will exclude gay and lesbian folks from becoming clergy and will further restrict the identity of those folks the Church has decided it can't affirm.

Have you had any negative reaction from the wider denomination for doing this?

No, we're very clear in saying that we're not starting United Methodist Churches. We're starting churches that see themselves as Wesleyan in terms of a lot of what is rich about the Methodist heritage--the quadrilateral, the organizational life, commitment to social justice, personal piety, but we're very clear that we're not starting United Methodist Churches. We are also talking about doing "extraordinary" ordinations. I've talked to some bishops who may participate in that. It would involve ordaining people who have met the criteria in every other way for ordination, but have been rejected or have been refused consideration because of their sexual orientation. It doesn't link them with a denomination. Obviously, if they are an openly gay or lesbian person trying to be ordained in the United Methodist Church, they'll be stopped. If we do these extraordinary ordinations they will not be ordained United Methodists, because there's a process for that. They will be ordained into this new tradition. We have found agreement to do this from one bishop and have had interest from other bishops. Probably our first ordination will be sometime after next April, maybe as early as next July. It will likely be an ecumenical ordination so there would be representatives from other denominations there. When asked about some of these concepts, I tell people that ever since the trial, I've been doing a ministry in the loopholes, things that are technically legal, and still do full ministry. That's the challenge.

For now, you are working hard to find ways to minister and to get past the boundaries being thrown up by the United Methodist policymakers. Do you see any hope for change in the traditional United Methodist Church system?

I think all the signs say it's going to get worse, and most of those reasons

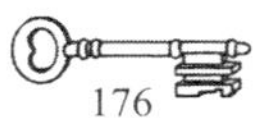

are demographic. I think there's an increasing likelihood that a schism will be entertained. There are people on both sides, so to speak, who resist that and there are people on both sides who see that as a possibility for us to get on with what we understand faithfulness to be. As a United Methodist, I believe that sometimes divorce is the most faithful thing a couple can do. It's the most life affirming and faith affirming thing, but it always has to be done with a sense of the tragedy, the loss and the grief that accompanies it. I don't know if the Church will formally split or if it will look at some other opportunities, but I think there are growing numbers of people--particularly since the recent Judicial Council decision--growing numbers of people who are saying this is going on too long. We have been beating each other up and beating ourselves up for too long and there are too many people who are "dying."

This is not an issue of some kind of philosophical debate. People are living and dying because of this. I have had too many people talk to me about their own suicide attempts, and that's got to stop. The Church is guilty of murder because of the way it has distorted the Gospel. I can't treat this as if it's some kind of ongoing process that takes time. People need ways to find their own healing, their own security, and I understand that, I support all that. But, as a pastor I see person after person come through this church, through these doors, scared to death to sit in the pew, then saying, "I was on my way to the lake," or "I was on my way to the drugstore to do myself in." That's got to stop.

Do you have particular scriptures that define your ministry or keep you going when it gets tough?

The story of creation when God does all of this amazing creation is my favorite. After every part of the diversity of creation, God says, "It is good!" That doesn't mean it can't get messed up, that we can't mess ourselves up and mess others up, but Creation is good. It's not so much about original sin as it's about original blessing. The attitude of Jesus, his whole ministry was so anti-institutional religion. He was a champion of the faith that broke the rules, not for the sake of breaking the rules, but for the sake of two stronger scriptural models--the whole ministry of Jesus with women, with Samaritans, with outcasts, and the declaration at the beginning of the Bible in which God declares Creation to be good.

Conclusion

The Key Ring

I thought I was finished with *Voices from the Kingdom.* I handed my finished collection of interviews to my good friend and ongoing pastor, Bill, after church one Sunday. I'd expected that he'd read it--perhaps do a critique of sorts--and then return it to me with an endorsement. He included his wife, Beverly, also a good friend of mine, in the project. During the break between Sunday school and Church several Sundays later, Bill handed me the body of work and said to me, "It's not finished! It needs another chapter."

I have to admit I was somewhat taken aback until he explained why he'd made that assessment.

"Beverly and I both felt like the book just ended. You need to reflect on what 'keys' we now hold as a result of reading these interviews."

To tell the truth, I had considered lifting up a few thoughts and insights that I'd personally drawn from the interviews, but thought it best if I let each reader do that for himself or herself. As I thought about it, I realized that they could still do that. Each reader would hear what was being said in accordance with his or her own faith background and life experience. I decided to take Bill and Beverly's advice and give it a try.

It seemed to me that the logical first step was to take a close look at the title, *Voices from the Kingdom: All God's Children Have Keys*. I decided to start with the main title, *Voices from the Kingdom.*

Words can be surprisingly revealing. In my digging through the dictionary and a thesaurus I found a fascinating combination of definitions to put to the title. By defining the word *voice* as "an opinion or wish" and then using it in the phrase "giving a voice to", I came up with the idea of "giving others the opportunity to voice their spiritual opinions." In one source the word *kingdom* was equated with the word *domain* which was defined as "a field of activity and influence". Could this mean that all of our voices and faith experiences are valuable in influencing the Kingdom of God becoming alive and active in our world?

All God's Children Have Keys. The meaning of the phrase "all of God's children" is fairly apparent. It means *all* of God's children. What about the word *keys*? Following the word *key* in the thesaurus was the word *passport*. When I looked up the word *passport* in the dictionary it was defined as "something that enables one to be admitted or accepted."

What are the keys or passports that open the doors, bringing about the Kingdom of God as Jesus described it? What attitudes and actions best help open the doors to the Kingdom of God, now and into eternity? Perhaps they could best be expressed in the way Jesus, himself, laid out some other important guidelines.

Blessed are those who have a generous theology, for they shall open the door to God's love.

Blessed are those who speak out in the name of justice on behalf of the oppressed, for they shall risk criticism and exclusion from their peers.

Blessed are those who teach little children that Jesus loves them, for they will lavish their own love on the children who they shepherd.

Blessed are those who hold on to the extravagant love of Jesus, for they will be sustained by their faith.

Blessed are those who rant and rail and cry out to God in their time of pain, for they shall hear God's voice.

Blessed are those who work tirelessly to open the doors of the Church to everyone, for they will provide the keys to a place to call "home".

Blessed are those who bare their souls to share stories of tragedy and personal faith so that others may be healed, for they shall find healing for themselves.

Blessed are those who find integrity by faithfully living who God created them to be, for they will provide courage to others.

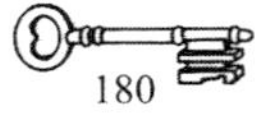

Blessed are they who risk paying attention to those who society calls outcasts, for they shall meet God's angels.

Blessed are those who listen for God's voice in their lives, for they shall be God's angels.

Blessed are those who look with new eyes at God's Holy Scriptures, for they will discover grace.

Blessed are those who risk bending the rules that get in the way of compassion, for they shall save lives.

Blessed are they who struggle to find a way to fulfill their spiritual callings, for they keep their relationship with God alive.

Now all I needed to do was put it all together to see if the title fit with what happened in the book. *Voices from the Kingdom: All God's Children Have Keys.* The faith stories that were told in this book gave voice to the wishes, opinions and experiences of a part of God's creation that isn't always heard or valued. These voices are an active and valuable influence in bringing about the Kingdom of God and, yes, all God's children have passports!

May it be so! Amen!

Beverly Cole is a wife, a mother, and a church woman. As Christian and the mother of a gay son, she has worked as an educator, an advocate, and a supporter for the gay community in society and in the Church. She works nationally with the Reconciling Parents Network of the United Methodist Church and is coordinator for that organization in the Kansas West Conference.

Beverly has told their family story to numerous church, university, professional and civic groups and has published her experience in Cleaning Closets: A Mother's Story. Cleaning Closets *has been featured on the United Methodist Women's international list of recommended reading for the Church.*

Kansas is home for Beverly, her husband, Dale, and their three cats, Smokey, Cassie, and Janet. Beverly enjoys spending time with her daughter, Traci, and traveling to visit her son, Eric, and his partner, Joe. In her spare time, she relaxes by reading, gardening and also hiking in places where her husband can capture nature with his camera.

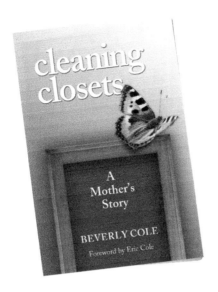

Religious Groups Supporting Open Faith Communities

Affirmation-Mormon
Affirmation
Gay and Lesbian Mormons
PO Box 46022
Los Angeles, CA 90046-0022
Phone-1-661-367-2421
www.affirmation.org

United Methodist Affirmation
Affirmation
United Methodists for Lesbian/Gay Concerns
PO Box 1021,
Evanston, IL 60204
umaffirmation@yahoo.com

American Baptists Concerned
American Baptists Concerned
PO Box 3183
Walnut Creek, CA 94598
www.rainbowbaptists.org

Brethren Mennonite Council for Gay Concerns
Brethren Mennonite Council for Gay Concerns
PO Box 6300
Minneapolis, MN 55406
Phone-1-612-343-2060
bmc@bmclgbt.org

Dignity (Catholic)
Dignity
1500 Massachusetts Ave NW
Suite 8
Washington DC 20005
Phone-1 800-877-8797
Phone-1-202-861-0017
info@dignityusa.org

Friends for Lesbian, Gay, Bisexual, Transgender, and Queer Concerns (Quaker)
Newsletter
c/o Sue Sierra
1314 Wright Street
Ann Arbor MI 48105
www.quaker.org/flgbtqc

GLAD Alliance-Gay and Lesbian Affirming Disciples (Disciples of Christ)
GLAD Alliance
PO Box 44400
Indianapolis, IN 46244-0400
glad@gladalliance.org

Integrity- (Episcopal)
Integrity
620 Park Ave # 311
Rochester, NY 14607-2943
Phone-1-800-462-9498
info@integrityusa.org

Lutherans Concerned/North America
Lutherans Concerned/North America
PO Box 4707
St. Paul, MN 55104-0707
Phone-1-651-665-0861
www.lcna.org/contact.shtm

Presbyterians for Lesbian/Gay Concerns
More Light Presbyterians
PMB 246
4737 County Rd. 101
Minnetanka, MN 55345-2634
www.mlp.org

Reconciling Ministries Network
(United Methodist)
3801 N Keeler Ave
Chicago IL 60641
Phone-1-773-736-5526
www.rmnetwork.org

Unitarian Universalist Office of
Lesbian/Gay Concerns
Unitarian Universalist Association
25 Beacon St
Boston, MA 02108
Phone- 1-617-742-2100
info@uua.org

Universal Fellowship of
Metropolitan Community Churches
MCC Churches
PO Box 691728
W. Hollywood, CA 90069
Phone- 1-310-360-8640
info@mccchurch.net